Confessions
behind
Closed Doors

Shanequa Lashay Anderson

confessionspublishing@yahoo.com

ISBN-10: 0615641288
EAN-13: 9780615641287
Library of Congress Control Number: 2012908232
confessions publication, Houston, TX

I dedicate this book to my beautiful daughter

HEAVEN FELICIA LEE MCCUIN

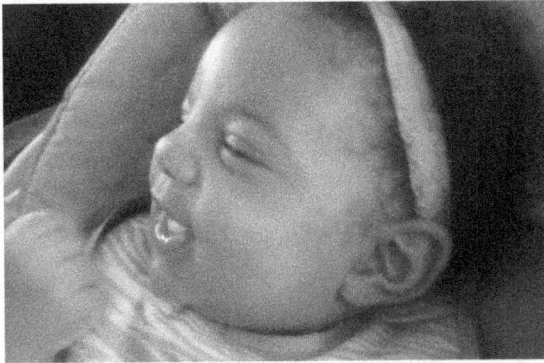

Acknowledgements

This has been an overwhelming and exciting experience for me. I began working on this book in February of 2011, and it has been an amazing journey. First I would love to say thank you to my beautiful and wonderful mother (Felicia Ann Anderson), you are truly an amazing mother, wife and friend. Without you I would not be here, and I strive every day to make you proud.

I also would like to thank my father (Michael Wayne Smith), I mean what can I say, you are my rock. Whenever I was down or in a rut, you would always come to my rescue without criticizing me for my mistake. Without you this would have not been possible for me to do.

And to my husband (Richard Lee McCuin), you are an amazing person; for the most part you have stood by my side and helped me get through some of the most difficult times in my life. I thank you for loving me and supporting my dreams. Last but not least I would like to thank god for blessing me with a beautiful daughter (Heaven Felicia Lee McCuin), she gives me the strength to keep going. She gave me the strength to finish my book and proceed with having it published.

I just want to thank you all, and I want for you all to know that this would not have been possible without you all support

THANK YOU
AND
I LOVE YOU ALL

Introduction

∂℘

Confessions by Cheri

DIRECTOR TOM: Cameras rolling in five, four, three, two. LaShay, you're on now.

LASHAY MARIEE: Hi, everyone. I'm your host LaShay Mariee. Thanks for tuning in for the very first episode of this jaw-dropping series, **Confessions Behind Closed Doors.** *This is the show where confessions are told and lives are changed—for better or for worse.*

Our first confessor is thirty-four-year-old Cheri Hathaway from Nashville, Tennessee. Cheri says that this secret has been suppressing her mental state of mind for some time now. Her ability to concentrate on reality began to weigh in on her. But she's here today to confess and open the doors for the world to know. Everyone, please welcome Miss Cheri Hathaway to the show.

*[*The audience applauds. The camera shifts to the silhouette and shadow behind the closed doors, where a jittery Cheri steps onto the stage.*]*

LASHAY MARIEE: So, Cheri, you do know that once you confess your story you must come from behind the closed doors and reveal who you are?

CHERI: Yes, LaShay, I do know that, but I don't care.

LASHAY MARIEE: So you're OK with that—I mean, OK with all the judgments everyone will make of you?

CHERI: I have to face this. There's no other option. [Cheri sniffles and sighs.] Holding this in has been unbearable. I'm ready.

LASHAY MARIEE: OK, Cheri, the floor is yours. When we come back from the break, you will hear Cheri Hathaway's heart-dropping story and what got her here to **Confessions Behind Closed Doors.**

DIRECTOR TOM: Cut. Everyone back on set in five minutes. LaShay, that was great. Keep up the good work.

LASHAY MARIEE: Wow, why is it so hot in here? I can't give my best under these conditions. That's enough. I said that's enough makeup, damn it! I don't want to look like a clown.

***

DIRECTOR TOM: OK, everyone, take your places please. Jeremy, dim light four over LaShay. Cameras rolling in five, four, three, two. LaShay, you're on now.

LASHAY MARIEE: Hi, everyone, I'm your host LaShay, and welcome back to **Confessions Behind Closed Doors.** *Up now and ready to tell it all is thirty-four-year old Cheri Hathaway, wife and mother from Nashville, Tennessee. Cheri, are you ready? Ready to tell the world your story?*

CHERI: Yes, LaShay, I am. I'm ready to get this off of my chest, and I know that the time is now.

LASHAY MARIEE: Well, Cheri, the floor is yours. Begin whenever you're ready.

CHERI: Well, hello, everyone. My name is Cheri Hathaway, and I have a "confession" that I have to get off my chest. [Cheri sniffles and sighs.]

LASHAY MARIEE: Cheri, it's OK. You can do this. Take your time.

CHERI: Well, about nine years ago, I met my husband, and I love him dearly. I really do love him. Well, when we met, he had already had a son from a previous marriage. His name is Dontae—Dontae Webster. He has his mother's last name, not his father's. When we met nine years ago, we were such a happy family. Everything was going great. It was just me, my husband, and Dontae all the time.

My husband got a new job on the east side, which was forty-five minutes away from our home. So I would have to take Dontae to school in the mornings, since my husband left so early for work now. Dontae and I began to bond so much on the twenty-minute ride to his school every morning. [Cheri sighs.]

LASHAY MARIEE: Cheri, it's OK. Take your time. We're here to listen.

CHERI: I just began to feel so much closer to him…like he was starting to think of me as his…well, as his mom. One night Joe, my husband, did not make it home on time. And all I can remember is calling him and calling him, just to get no answer. Finally, he called me back, and he said, and I quote: "Honey, I'll be working late tonight, real late. So I'm just going to spend the night at the office." Suddenly I heard a woman's voice say in a seductive manner, "Joe, come back to bed, baby." Then all I heard was the dial tone. [Cheri sniffles.] From all I knew, he didn't even have an office It was more of a cubicle.

LASHAY MARIEE: Cheri, hold that thought. We have to take a little break, but when we return, Cheri will continue her stand to confess the untold in her life. Don't go anywhere. We'll be right back after the following messages.

DIRECTOR TOM: LaShay, that was amazing. Everyone, please make your way back to the set in ten minutes.

LASHAY MARIEE: OK, well, I'm going to my dressing room. I need a cigarette. Billy, please can you get that for me? Yes, Shay I'll get it just go to your dressing room. I'll bring it to you.

***

"LaShay, we need you back on the set. We're on in three minutes."

"Damn, I just got in my dressing room. Can I at least get a twenty-minute break?"

***

DIRECTOR TOM: Everyone, take your places please. OK, LaShay, we're on in five, four, three, two. We're on now.

LASHAY MARIEE: Hello there. I'm your host LaShay. And before we went to break, Cheri Hathaway was in the middle of her confession. Cheri, would you like to proceed with your confession?

CHERI: Yes, LaShay, I would like to. Well, like I was saying before break, I didn't even know he had an office. So when I heard that woman's voice and then he hung up the phone right after that, I knew he was cheating. I knew. It was so obvious.

LASHAY MARIEE: Wow, Cheri. And how did that make you feel, knowing what he was out doing and you're waiting at home?

CHERI: That made me very upset, LaShay. I was pissed off. So I did not call him back. I just sat there in our room by the fireplace, crying, just crying. All of a sudden I heard the room door open, and when I looked up, it was Dontae. [Cheri pauses and takes a deep breath.]

LASHAY MARIEE: Cheri, why is this so hard for you to do...to confess?

CHERI: Because, LaShay, this should have never happened. I'm so disappointed in myself and what I stood for at that point in time. When Dontae came in the room, I was in Joe's tank top, one that he had outgrown. It had his favorite football team on it—the Saints, and some lace black panties. But when Dontae came into the room, he looked past all of that. I mean, it didn't feel like he even knew I was sitting there half naked. He had on those muscle shirts the boys wear and a pair of black Jordan basketball shorts.

Dontae came to sit by me, and when he did, he put his hand on my thigh and told me that it was going to be OK. He said he knew why I was crying, we both looked at each other, deep in one another's eyes, then I leaned in and kissed him. I kissed Dontae! *At that time Dontae was sixteen and I was thirty-three.*

[The audience boos.]

CHERI: One thing led to another, and the next thing I know, we—me and Dontae—were in me and Joe's bed, making love as if it was me and Joe.

LASHAY MARIEE: Cheri, is this true? Is this really true? I mean, he's your stepson, your husband's blood.

CHERI: [Cheri whispers] Yes, LaShay, it is true, but I really wish it wasn't. He made me feel young all over again that night. For the next couple of weeks, Dontae and I continued to have these little sessions when his dad left for work in the mornings. Well, to make an even longer story short, I just recently had a baby girl her name is Jessica Webster. When I decided to give her the same last name as Dontae, I knew why, but my husband did not. So I gave him this lame excuse that it would make Dontae feel closer to the baby, but it was really because it's Donates baby. I mean, the dates matched up perfectly.

LASHAY MARIEE: Cheri, are you serious? Is that really the truth?

CHERI, Yes, LaShay, it is. And I know my family and my husband will see this. I'm sorry. I want to tell them all that I'm really sorry.

LASHAY MARIEE: Wow, Cheri. Well, please come from behind the closed doors. It's time for you to put the face with the confession. Open the doors please.

[The doors open, and out steps thirty-four-year-old Cheri Hathaway, an African American woman about five foot nine, 125 pounds, and red, shoulder-length hair. The audience boos.]

LASHAY MARIEE: Well, Cheri, how do you feel now that you've con-fessed and opened up the doors to your life?

CHERI: LaShay, I feel great, but I'm a little afraid about what's going to happen when I go home.

*LASHAY MARIEE: Well, Cheri, we all wish you luck with whatever happens. Please keep the show up to date with your transition, Cheri, and thanks for coming on the show. [**The camera shifts to LaShay**] I'm your host LaShay, and this has been the first episode of* **Confessions Behind Closed Doors.**

Chapter 1

❧

The Host LaShay/The Person LaShay Mariee

"So what time does the next show start, Billy? Well, just call me back when you find out. OK bye-bye."

[LaShay walks in to her kitchen and opens the refrigerator.]

I'm so hungry, but every time I put a piece of food in my mouth, those fucking producers are down my throat. Damn, there's no more milk. Fuck it, I'm ordering Chinese. Where's the phone book? I know I laid it around here somewhere. Oh, there it is.

"Yes, I would like to place an order for delivery. My address is Four-Twenty-Five Ford Huntington Street, . Yes, I would like two of your veggie egg rolls and shrimp lo mein. Oh, and also a Diet Coke. No, that will be all. I will pay cash. Thank you."

My name is LaShayMariee, and I'm the host of the new show **Confessions Behind Closed Doors.** *On the show I use the name Shay. I don't know why, but I know I like it that way much better. I am five eleven. I weigh about 130 pounds, and I'm the biggest "fashionista" ever known. I love music, and I love my alone time.*

Today is my chill day, then back to work early tomorrow morning at five thirty. I got this job and fame through beauty pageants. They finally paid off in 2002 when I won the Miss America Pageant. I had no clue that in the audience was the producer and owner of a huge TV production company. He was about to produce five new shows, and he wanted me to host one of them. I guess that pageant really worked out in my favor.

[The doorbell rings.]

"Coming! Wait one moment please."

"That will be thirty-four ninety-five."

1

"Damn, you guys are expensive. Wait one moment. I have to get the money. Here you go. Keep the change."

"Thank you, ma'am. And you have a great day."

"You have a great day too, sir."

Shit, let me turn this up. I need to hear this.

Another killing in the Beverly Hills area. Same MO says the Beverly Hills Police Department. We advise all pedestrians to stay safe indoors and avoid any outside contact. We don't know when he or she will strike again."

Shit, they'll never find him or, for that matter, her. Let me get dressed and get out. Today is my day, and I'm not going to worry my mind about work. I need to get my nails done, my hair done, and I'm going partying in my new outfit.

[LaShay takes a couple of bites of shrimp lo Mein and dashes out the house with her keys, and purse in her hands.]

***

[It's 10:00 p.m. LaShay arrives back home.]

Bath, then straight to bed for me. All I need now is some bubble bath, a little Keith Sweat, and my waterproof vibrator. It feels so good to be in the bath. I had such a great and relaxing day.

[LaShay slips down in her tub with her vibrator on full blast.]

***

[The alarm goes off.]

Oh my God! It's ten thirty a.m. I thought I set it for nine a.m. Damn it. Move, Cha-Cha.

[LaShay's phone rings.]

"Hello. Hey, Billy. I know I'm late. I set the alarm clock an hour late, but I'm on my way now. OK, just tell them I will be on set in thirty minutes. I'm on my way. All right. Bye."

***

"Tell the set Shay is pulling up now in garage four."

"Hey Billy, I just wanted to ask you are the producers upset with me being late?"

"Hey, Shay. Unfortunately, yes, the producers are very upset."

"Well, you know what Billy? Fuck them. I have damn near made this show what it is up to this very day. You know that Billy."

"Yes, Shay believe me, I do know that. You really have."

"They still don't give me any kind of leeway with the company—even after all that I've done."

"Calm down, Shay. Just go talk to them and tell them how you feel about everything."

"Billy, that's all I ever do is talk to them. Just forget about it Billy. I'll be fine. So where's the script for today? Who's the confessor? Isn't it that lady RoseMery?"

"Yes, I think so Shay, but we have five minutes until you have to be on set, OK?"

"OK Billy, I'll be right there. Please send in Cacey and Briana. Please hurry you guys, I have to be on set in less than five minutes."

"OK Shay, all done, and you look great."

"Thanks you guys. Wish me luck."

[Shay dashes on to the set.]

"OK, I'm finally finished. So where is RoseMery? I want to go say hi to her. Well, I really want to go feel her out a little bit."

"OK, you go do that. We're on in two minutes, Shay."

"Hi, RoseMery. My name is—"

"Wait! You don't even have to say your name. I know who you are. You're LaShay …well, LaShayMariee. I always watch your show, and it's an honor to finally meet you."

"Well RoseMery, thank you so much, I really appreciate your support. So are you ready to tell your confession and let the world know your story?"

"Yes Shay I am. I mean, it's now or never."

"You are so right about that."

***

3

DIRECTOR TOM: Everyone to the set. We're on in five minutes.

OK, everyone take your places and please do a touch up on Shay. Cameras rolling in five, four, three, two. Shay, you're on now.

LASHAY MARIEE: Hello, everyone I'm your fabulous host LaShay Mariee. Welcome to another crazy, jaw-dropping episode of **Confessions Behind Closed Doors.** *Today we have RoseMery Johnson as our confessor—a twenty-three-year-old motivational speaker from Houston, Texas. RoseMery, are you ready to confess…confess to the truth?*

ROSEMERY: Yes, LaShay I am, but only because I know that my story will touch and help someone else in the world. So that makes me feel much better about the whole ordeal.

LASHAY MARIEE: Yes RoseMery, you definitely will help millions of people just by sharing your story. So, RoseMery, just start whenever you're ready, and remember to just take your time.

ROSEMERY: OK, LaShay I'm ready. Well I'm Rose, and I'm twenty-three years old. I was born and raised in Houston, Texas, on the grimy streets of South Acres Homes. Half of my mother's pregnancy with me, she was taking methadone and smoking crack. So when I was born I immediately had convulsions and I had seizures followed by very intense headaches. When I was about nine, my mom met this guy—huh, and **some** *guy he was.*

LASHAY MARIEE: RoseMery, what do you mean by that…that he was **some** *guy? Because I heard you put emphasis on that.*

ROSEMERY: Well I mean, that he wasn't in that house—my mom's house. Shit, my house that I'm supposed to feel safe in at that age. He wasn't in there but five minutes before he started trying to show me how to be a woman. "But don't tell Mommy," he would say. "Just let her see how great of a woman you're growing up to be."

LASHAY MARIEE: You were so young Rose. How did that affect you? I mean, I know you were young at the time—very young. I do have to say, Rose, that is very horrid.

ROSEMERY: Yes LaShay, it is very horrid. At that time I did not know what to do. I didn't want to play with my friends or go to school. My mom relapsed on drugs after I was only five, and by then I was nine. It had been four years, and she was still doing the methadone. She'd do crack occasionally. So while she was in the room with his drugs—oh yeah, he was a drug dealer. One of the biggest across the board. He was our main source of income.

Our welfare checks and food stamps were really all we had before he came into the picture, my mom would say to me sometimes. Around the age of thirteen, I began getting into a lot of trouble, involving myself with heavy and illegal drugs and alcohol. I cannot believe by the time I was fifteen—well, I recall me being around the age of fourteen or fifteen. Anyways, I could not believe by that time my mom and I were arguing over whose turn it was to take the next hit.

I mean, it was crazy. She was crazy. "Rose is you OK back there?" she'd ask. "Is everything fine?" How can you do something like that to your only daughter? I just don't understand how you could do that to someone you call your little princess. Well, by time I was seventeen, I was dancing and shaking my ass for nickels and dimes, doing cocaine at clubs. I was thinking that I was the hottest thing and I was grown. Please! I had no education and could not tell you what ten divided by three was if my life depended on it.

[The audience laughs.]

ROSEMERY: About time I turned eighteen, something came over me, and I just got back on track. Well, I met this guy, and he helped get me back on the right track. His name is Tony, and I love him so much.

LASHAY MARIEE: Do you really love him Rose, or could it just be lust?

ROSEMERY: Yes, LaShay I do. He's my man, and I'm his woman.

LASHAY MARIEE: How does he make you feel, Rose?

ROSEMERY: He makes me feel wonderful. But most of all, LaShay, he makes me feel safe and secure. He's really helped me turn my life around. I mean, now I have a high school diploma, and I'm in my third year of college, going for my fourth year.

LASHAY MARIEE: Oh! And Rose, what are you majoring in, if I might ask?

ROSEMERY: Oh, I'm going for psychotherapy, and I think that goes great with what I'm doing now and absolutely love to do. I'm a motivational speaker.
    [The audience applauds.]

ROSEMERY: Thank you so much. I go around to schools, seminars, fundraiser banquets, and many more motivational events to speak about abuse, drugs, and how to deal with everyday life after going through different types of abuse. I've also just written a book called **Get Over It and Move On.** *It's mainly about individuals moving on with their lives and getting over things that they can't change instead of continuing to hang on to these things.*

LASHAY MARIEE: Wow, Rose, that's amazing and so inspiring to hear from such a young woman. I mean, Rose, you overcame it all and made something out of yourself in the end. How does it feel to have that accomplishment?

ROSEMERY: Well, LaShay, I just have a lot of faith in God and in myself.

LASHAY MARIEE: Well, everyone, when we return from the break, RoseMery Johnson will come from behind those closed doors to put the face with the confession. Rose, are you ready for this? Ready to show the world who you really are?

ROSEMERY: Yes, LaShay I am.

LASHAY MARIEE: Don't know about the rest of you, but I can't wait to see who's behind those doors.

DIRECTOR TOM: Break. LaShay, that was great. Back to set in five minutes.

***

"I need a cigarette in my dressing room, like right now, Billy!"
"OK Shay. I'm already two steps ahead of you. Here you go."
"Thanks Billy. Honey, you always know what I want."
[LaShay shuts the door to her dressing room and lights her cigarette.]
"Hello. Hi baby. What are you doing? Oh, that sounds great. I wish I was there with you, but I'm on set right now, taking my break. I get off at around four o'clock. Let's hook up then."

I bet you're wondering who I'm talking to. Well, his name is Jamie Lamont Jackson, Businessman of the Year. And he's my man. Lamont and I met about three years ago in Miami for a photo shoot for the most influential people in the world, with Essence magazine. He asked my publicist to get me in to help promote his big business launch of the year. He was there—all six feet of him was there. A body out of this world. **[LaShay smirks and giggles.]** *I love him so damn much.*

"Well, baby, I have to go now. They're calling me back to set. OK, I love you too, baby. Bye-bye."

***

DIRECTOR TOM: OK, everyone, take your places, please. And Billy, position LaShay on camera three. Everyone, cameras rolling in five, four, three, two. LaShay smile. You're on now.

LASHAY MARIEE: Welcome back. Just before we left for break, Rose-Mery Johnson was telling her amazing story of overcoming the odds and had accepted to come from behind closed doors and open the doors to her life. Rose, are you ready to show the world who you are. and put your face with your confession?

ROSEMERY: Yes LaShay. I am a little scared, but I'm ready.

LASHAY MARIEE: OK, open the doors and let her come out now, please.
    [The doors open. Out steps RoseMery Johnson, a tall, five foot eleven, pale Caucasian woman who is skinny with long brown hair and dark blue, dreamy eyes. The audience applauds.]

LASHAY MARIEE: Wow, Rose! You're beautiful—I mean, you're gorgeous!

ROSEMERY: Thank you LaShay, so very much.

LASHAY MARIEE: I mean, how is it you could go through something like that, something so cruel? It must have been so hard for you to come out of that.

ROSEMERY: Well LaShay, all I can say is that everyone goes through things in life, and God puts you through things for mysterious reasons.

LASHAY MARIEE: Thank you so very much Rose, for coming to the show and sharing your amazing story and confessing it to us all. You look absolutely stunning, and please keep the show up to date with your business.

ROSEMERY: No, thank you LaShay. I really appreciate it. This has been such a relieving experience. Oh, and my new book, Get Over It and Move On, *is out in your local book stores today. It's a wonderful read, and I recommend everyone to read it, I mean it's amazing.*

LASHAY MARIEE: But guess what? RoseMery is so generous to give all of us today in the studio audience a free copy of her first book, **Get Over It and Move On.**

[The audience applauds.]

LASHAY MARIEE: Well, thank you so much Rose, for coming to the show and sharing your confession with us—also for these amazing copies of your book.

ROSEMERY: No, LaShay, thank you for allowing me to come on the show and share it with you all.

LASHAY MARIEE: Well, this has been another crazy, yet heart-warming episode of **Confessions Behind Closed Doors.** *Thanks for tuning in with the studio audience. Please stay tuned to find out who's our next week's confessor.*

NEXT WEEK ON CONFESSIONS BEHIND CLOSED DOORS...

LASHAY MARIEE: Debra Jenkins, a year-old mother and wife from Oakland, California, with a confession that will tell the world how her daughter really died. Tune in next week to hear it all from Debra herself.

DIRECTOR TOM: Cut. OK, everyone, that was great. The producers want to have a meeting with all of you this Thursday to discuss changes in the show, so everyone make sure to be here and on time—seven a.m., sharp!

***

"Shay, I need to get you your notes for Thursday on Debra Jenkins."

"OK Billy, just drop it of at my house. You still have the spare key, right?"

"Yeah girl I do. So I'll be by to drop it of at around six-ish. Will that be fine?"

"Yeah, that's fine. Just stop by any time before eight."

"So how's everything going with you and your hunk of a man Lamont?"

"It's going great. We're trying to hang in there. Every relationship has its ups and downs. So how are you and Peaches doing?"

"Well, we're doing fine, but he's still struggling with the fact that we can't get married. So everything's great on my part."

"Billy, you and Peaches both just have to understand that a lot of couples have struggled with wanting to get married in the gay community—men and women. You both just have to hang in there and know that you're married at heart."

"I know that Shay, and I see it the same way you do. I just wish Peaches would see it the same way."

"Billy, can I ask you a crazy but serious question?"

"Of course Shay. What is it, girl?"

"Well, do you ever get the feeling like someone's following you—like spying on you? I know it sounds crazy, but I've been feeling like this for a while now."

"Shay, you're being silly. Go home."

Chapter 2

❧

The Everyday Me

"Wait. I will be right there. Don't go anywhere." Lamont jumped in his Jag with his heart on his sleeve and his life flashing before his eyes.

"Hello Lamont. Nice of you to be on time," said the woman behind the dark sunglasses. "You know, Mr. Jackson, these are some very exposing photos that I have here of you cheating on your little starlet girlfriend."

"How do I know you have any pictures of me doing anything? And for that matter, how do I know that you know who my girl is anyway? Why am I even here with you in the first place? I'm Jamie Lamont Jackson, Businessman of the Year. Bye. I don't have time for this type of mess."

"Mr. Jackson!" the woman shouted with a gun pointed to Jackson's head as she tossed the envelope filled with pictures. "Unless I hear from you within seventy-two hours, Mr. Jackson, an e-mail of those very photos will be sent out to every big network in the country. I tell you Mr. Jackson, I will get my money one way or the other. Although, you cooperating will be the preferred way. This is LaShays bestfriend, what do you think people aren't going to care about you cheating on your girlfriend with her best friend? Either way, I'm getting paid. "

"So how do I know you will give me all the copies and originals?"

"Well, I guess we'll be friends for a long time, Mr. Jackson. The pleasure has been all mines, Mr. Jackson." The woman slipped out the back door, pointing her gun and saying, "Don't follow me Jackson, or I will kill you."

Lamont opened the envelope and took out the pictures. While sitting down slowly, his heart jumping, blood racing, he said quietly in one

13

breath, *"Oh my God Shay's going to kill me if she sees this."* The tears rolled from his eyes.

"Are you on your way over here?"

"Yes Shay. I'm on my way now; I'll be pulling up in about five minutes."

"OK, well hurry up and get here. I've been waiting for you."

***

[Lamont quietly opens Shay's door and walks into her condo.]

"Hey, boo I'm here. Where you at?"

"I'm in here baby, I'm washing clothes. Come and give me a kiss."

[Shay and Lamont exchange a juicy, tongue-tied kiss.]

"So baby, how's everything with the show going?"

"It's going great, but I've been feeling a little weird lately."

"What do you mean a little weird?"

"I don't know Lamont—like someone's been following me or spying on me. It's probably nothing."

"Yeah boo, you're becoming somewhat of a star, and you're going to start getting that paranoid feeling."

"OK, you're right, baby. Give me a kiss. You're so right."

"What are we doing tonight baby? I'm a little bored."

"I don't know, but tomorrow I have to get up at six a.m. for a photo shoot. Oh, that reminds me, I need to call Billy and check to see if he's on point about everything. Put on a movie baby, and pop some popcorn while I call him."

"All right boo, just hurry up. We need to catch up on all of our missed out time with each other."

"Hi Billy honey, what time exactly is the photo shoot tomorrow? Are you sure it's at eight thirty? OK, well have a limo here to pick me up in the morning, OK? Bye, good night to you too. OK, baby, I'm done, did you put on the movie and pop the popcorn?"

"Yes sweetie I did. Now come get your sexy ass in bed with me. I've been missing you like crazy these last two months."

"You're so silly Lamont. So how have things been going with you and your promoting?"

"It's been going fine; it's just this deal that I've been trying to close for the last three months. It's been so exhausting trying to put this together, and get an actual offer set in stone."

"Well, who is it that you're trying to close the deal with?"

"This dude. His name is Khle Abob Johan. He's from India, and his dad is looking to open up a chain of nightclubs and diners. He wants his son to manage them all, and I'm the promoter. They're just so damn picky, and it's really starting to piss me off."

"Well, baby just keep at it. And remember, all you can do is give it your all. Don't beat yourself up about it. I know you're going to close the deal."

"Thanks baby, you always know how to cheer me up. Now let's go to sleep."

***

[LaShay's alarm clock goes off, and her cell phone rings.]

Hello? Yes Billy, I'm up. OK. I'm on my way. Just give me about twenty minutes to get dressed. All right. Bye-bye. Baby, I'm about to get dressed and go. Are you coming with me?" No boo, I'm not going to be able to make this photo shoot. I'm sorry, but I can't."

"Well, will you be able to at least stop by when you get up and get dressed?"

"I can't, baby. I told you last night about that big deal I have to close today—or try to close."

"Oh, I forgot about that baby. I'm sorry."

"Yeah, I have to close that deal—especially if my baby wants that new custom Maserati I've been hearing about for the last two months."

***

"Damn, Billy where is LaShay at?"
"She'll be here shortly. Just give her a little time."
"Shay, girl, where you at?"

"I'm at the light across the street from the set. I'll be there in less than two minutes. Hold on."

***

"LaShay's here. Tell everyone on set she's finally here."

[LaShay **rushes into the building and on to the set of the photo shoot.**]

"Hi everyone, sorry I'm so late. That damn traffic is crazy out there."

"OK, that's fine LaShay, but we really need you in your first outfit like ten minutes ago—and hair and makeup right after."

"Everyone, we are one hour behind schedule. We need to move a little faster people."

"OK, LaShay, I need you over there in the chair for your makeup."

"So are there going to be doubles made of all the pictures, because I need to take copies of all of them for my portfolio."

"Yes, I think they are. But if they're not making copies, we can get them made for you if you need them. Shay, I need you to make your way in your first outfit, doll."

"Oh, Billy, I love this outfit. Don't you? It's so gorgeous."

"That is beautiful girl—especially the sequence in it. And you know I love sequence. Shay, it will fit you perfectly, but I'm sorry to say that's not your first outfit. This one is. So go and get dressed now, please. We are really behind schedule."

"OK Billy. Get off your period, honey. Calm down. I mean, who's the star here? I am. Shit, I'm worth way more than what they're paying me, and they're only paying me a hundred thousand. I mean, damn."

***

"Are you ready to go on set now?"

"Yes, I'm ready. Let's get this shit over with."

***

" Now let's get the hell out of here, I parked the car out front."

"Fuck, I'm so happy that photo shoot is over Billy. I hate to ask, but what's on my schedule next?"

"Well, Shay, at around three thirty you have to make that radio appearance at Ninety-Seven Nine The Box, and you have to go to Club Barrio at around eight p.m. That's about it. Today was a smooth day, but tomorrow it's back to work for you."

"Well, then I'm just going to take a couple moments out to call Lamont and let him know I'm going to be out a little later than I thought."

"Shay, call your man girl. If he was my man I'd be calling him back to back to back every day, sweetie. Every day."

"I bet you would Billy. You're so silly."

"Hey baby, what are you doing? That sounds good. I wish I was there. I'm not doing anything now, just left the photo-shoot getting in the car with Billy. Yes we just left, but I was calling to let you know I'm going to be working a little later than I hoped. Billy just went over my schedule with me, and I have to go to Club Barrio tonight. I'm sorry. Oh, baby, thanks for understanding, I love you so much, and I wanted to ask you: how did the deal go? Did you close it? Remember the deal you told me you wanted to close today? With that guy from India? Congratulations baby. I'm so proud of you. I knew you could do it. So if I might ask, how much did you close the deal for? Damn boo, that's a hell of a commission! Shit, I don't even need to work tonight, fucking with your checkbook. Well, I love you baby, but I have to go now. Oh and don't forget, I want my Maserati in black."

"So, how much did he make?"

"What are you talking about? My conversation on the phone?"

"Yes, bitch you know what I'm talking about. Don't play tramp. You already have his checkbook; your ass could at least tell me the limit sometimes."

"Damn, Billy he made twenty-five million off of this deal he just closed with these Arabs from India."

"Damn Shay. Now that's what I'm talking about. The type of numbers that get a bitch pussy wet. Man girl, I wish I was making that kind of money for me and Peaches. Shit, but I'm not even making close to it."

"I'm so proud of him Billy. He's worked so hard for this, and I really think he deserves it."

"I know, Shay. He treats you so good. You both deserve everything you have. Well, we're here girl, and it's packed as hell."

"OK. Just call the owner and tell him we're here now."

"Hi Mannie. This is Billy. Yes, LaShay Mariee's assistant. I just wanted to inform you that we've just pulled up in the back entrance of the club. OK, we'll be waiting."

***

"Hi LaShay. It's very nice to meet you. My name is Mannie. Welcome to Club Barrio."

"Oh, hi, Mannie. It's very nice to meet you also. So it seems pretty packed in there. Is it like this all the time?"

"Hell yeah. It's always packed in Mannie's spot, but it's especially like this tonight since the beautiful LaShay Mariee is here."

"You're so sweet Mannie. Well, let's get this damn party started."

"You haven't said anything but a word. Just follow me this way.

OK, LaShay, you just stand right here. I'm going to announce that you've just arrived.

[Mannie walks on stage.]

"What's up, ya'll? It's your boy, Mannie."

[The crowd applauds.]

"I want ya'll to make some motherfucking noise for this sexy- independent woman I'm about to bring out here to party with us. Welcome LaShayMariee to the stage."

[The crowd applauds.]

"Hey, what's going down, Club Barrio? How ya'll doing tonight? Well, let's get this party started. And for the next thirty-five minutes, drinks are on me. So if you're not trying to spend, make your way to the bar. First come, first serve. And somebody please pass me a drink."

***

[Five hours later.]
"OK, Shay, it's time to go. Are you ready?"
"Yes, I'm ready. Let's get the hell out of here. I'm so fucking tired, it's crazy. Well, Billy, it was a great night, but I'm really tired, so I'm just going to go home and take a bath, then straight to bed for me."
"OK, you do that. Peaches is calling me to come home, so I guess I'm going home to do the same. Just call me in the morning so we can go over your schedule."

***

[LaShay's cell phone rings.]
"Hey baby. Well, so-called baby. Why haven't you been picking up your phone for me, Lamont? So you're telling me you haven't received any of my calls? Yeah right, Lamont; you're such a fucking liar. I know this much. When you get to my condo, and I don't see any missed calls from me, we're going to have a problem. What do you mean, why? You know why. Because that means you deleted my calls. For what, I don't know, but you need to let me know why."
[LaShay hangs up her phone.]
Ugh, I swear that nigga thinks I'm so dumb. He has another thing coming.

***

[Three hours later, Lamont opens the door and walks quietly into LaShay's condo.]
"Can I see your phone now, please?"
"Damn, boo, you scared me; I thought you would be gone to bed by now. And why are you sitting in the dark."
"Well, Lamont, you thought wrong. I was just sitting here thinking about the lies you were going to try and tell me. Now let me see your phone."
"Baby, you're really tripping. Stop treating me like a child baby. I don't do you like that."

"OK. And Lamont, I still want to see your phone. I mean, damn, you can see mine too. I have nothing at all to hide."

[Shay and Lamont exchange phones.]

"I hope you're happy now, Shay."

"See, you're a fucking liar, Lamont. You deleted all the missed calls from me."

"OK, baby I lied. But don't trip. It's not that serious. I'm sorry. OK, baby? I'm sorry. It won't happen again."

"You know what, Lamont? This time sorry doesn't work; you need to tell me why you did that."

"Damn baby. It was because you were calling me and calling me while I was in a meeting, boo."

"Lamont, honey, you're going to have to come up with something better than that."

"Shay, I swear I'm telling you the truth. Don't just shut me down like that."

"OK, Lamont, if you say so. If you're spending the night, you need to grab a blanket and a pillow, because I refuse to let you sleep with me."

"Now you're crossing the line, Shay. I'm not sleeping on a damn couch. Now you're tripping."

"Well, go sleep in your own damn bed, because you're not sleeping in mine."

[Lamont storms out of LaShay's condo.]

"I can't stand your ass, Shay! I really can't stand you!"

"I can't stand your ass either, you prick. Come on, Cha-Cha. Come get in bed with mama. Daddy's tripping right now."

[LaShay cuddles next to her puppy Cha-Cha, and holds him tight like he was Lamont]

"Hey, Maria girl what are you doing? Uh, you're so nasty, but whatever. I'm just laying here in bed with Cha-Cha. Girl, I'm so pissed off with Lamont's ass right now. I really don't want to talk about him. Because he's such a compulsive liar. I mean, he lies about everything. So let's just change the subject. What are you doing tomorrow? Oh, that's nice. Are you doing anything tomorrow after eight in the evening time?

Well, do you want to go and chill somewhere with me? My treat! I don't know, I was thinking maybe we could go and get manis and pedis at this new spa I go to. OK that sounds great, girl. Just call me when you're ready for me to come and get you. All right. Bye."

***

[Billy's alarm clock goes off.]
"Billy, baby, wake up. The alarm clock is going off. Time for you to get up."

"I know Peaches. I just need ten more minutes of sleep, baby."

"Well, do you want anything for breakfast when you do get up?"

"Yeah, please sweetheart. Some pancakes and eggs. Oh, baby, did Shay call me this morning?"

"No, not that I know of anyway. Check your phone."

"I don't see it boo. Can you pass it too me? Well, I guess today is my rest day."

"Why you say that, you know you almost never get a rest day. I thought you told me you had to work all this week."

"I thought I did to, but Shay texted me an hour ago, saying for me to relax today because she's going to be out with Maria all day. I hate that bitch Maria. I swear she's up to no good with Lamont. But Shay just won't listen to me."

"Baby, well that's nice she gave you today off. Don't spoil it. Let Shay worry about Shay. She's a grown woman. OK Billy?"

"You're right, baby. I'm spending time with you today. Come here and give me a kiss. It's just that I feel like I'm stuck in between because Shay's just not my boss, she's my best friend. And I would never want anything to happen to her."

"Well, look baby just stop worrying yourself. Shay is my friend to, but I'm pretty sure she has Lamont's ass in check.

"Are you still going to make my breakfast, baby?"

"Yes, Billy I am. You can stop asking me."

"Well, while you're doing that, I'm going to make a couple of calls to the producers."

"Hello. Hi Tom, this is Billy. I just wanted to go over LaShay's schedule with you. Well, what confessor is on Thursday? Debra. OK, what time is the run-through for the Thursday show? That's good. And what time does she need to be there for hair and makeup? Thanks Tom, for your time. I will make sure to let LaShay know about the schedule."

[Billy hangs up the phone with Tom, and waits for his breakfast] "Peaches, please tell me the food is done. I'm hungry baby."

"Yes Billy it's almost done. Come sit down at the table. I'm about to fix your plate."

"Thanks sweetie it looks amazing. Oh! And I wanted us to get out today; you know go and spend some time together."

"I think I'm just going to jump in the shower first and get dressed. Let's go shopping today, baby; I don't have to work, so it'll be fun."

***

[One hour later.]

"Peaches, let's go. You don't need all that makeup on. You look amazing without it, baby."

"Billy, wait. And stop rushing me all the time. Go and start the car."

"All right, I'm going, but hurry your but hurry your ass up."

"Whatever, Billy. You'd better calm your ass down."

"Damn, Peaches. What took you so long?"

"I had to put on my eyeliner and change shirts, baby. Look, I'm in the car now so just drive. So what's been going on with you and Shay at these clubs?"

"Nothing much. She just makes her appearance at the club, and we chill out there for a while. The other night we went to Club Barrio. It was cool, but some dude was up there tripping trying to fuck with Shay. The bodyguard was about to fuck him up, but Shay told him not to. Shit, not me though. If I was her, I would have let him fuck that dude's world up. Other than that, everything's been going great. Even the show is doing very well."

"Oh, that's great boo. I'm so proud of you. I know that you've been working hard."

"Oh, and I got a twenty-dollar raise, so now I'm making fifty-five dollars an hour."

"Oh really? So why haven't you told me this?"

"I just did tell you. That's why I'm taking my boo-boo shopping."

"Well, you should have told me sooner. I've been wanting to shop."

"I'm sorry baby. I know I should have told you. It won't happen again boo. We're here. Let's go shopping now baby. Peaches, you look great. Get out of the mirror, and let's go shopping."

"So, what's our spending limit?"

"Well, Peaches, just know that I'm not Shay. I'm Shay's assistant. So we do have somewhat of a budget. We can spend about forty thousand. Is that good enough for you?"

"Yes, daddy, it is. Give me a kiss. I want to go in Sacks first baby. Oh, baby smell this perfume. Doesn't it smell amazing?"

"If you like it, then buy it, baby."

"OK, let's just take this stuff to the counter, then we can go to the next store."

"Your total will be three thousand dollars and forty-three cents. Will you be paying with cash or a credit card?"

"We will be paying with cash, ma'am."

"OK, thank you. Have a great day."

"Now let's go over there to that store, baby."

***

[Five hours later.]

"OK, boo, get the bags out of the car."

"Help me get the bags; just don't leave me out here to get them on my own. Over half of this stuff in here is yours."

***

"Girl, thanks for taking me out today. I really needed this after messing around with Brent's ass."

"Why Maria? What bullshit are you letting him put you through now?"

"Shay, he's just always out late, and I know he's out messing around with these triflin' hoes."

"Girl, he's not any different than Lamont's ass. We just got into a fight the other night over the same kind of shit. But that's just how men are."

"Well, Shay, I feel like I can't be mad at him, in a way though."

"Why can't you? I feel like you have every right to be."

"Because I know that I have my ways also. I know that he has probably cheated on me, but that's OK because I've cheated on him also."

"Maria, what the hell is wrong with you? You can't be serious right now."

"Yes, I'm serious, bitch. And don't act like you have never ever cheated on Lamont—I mean, with all the shit he puts you through."

"No, Maria. And let me stop you right there, bitch. I have never cheated on my man, and I don't need to. If anything, I think he's cheating on me."

"Girl, Lamont loves you. Stop wanting your life to be fucked. Bitch, I wish my life was like yours."

"So where is Brent right now?"

"I don't know. Probably with one of his other females. I tried to call him, but I got sent to voice mail. He wouldn't even pick up for the nanny's number when she called. So fuck him. He can literally go to hell.

"Why do you think men are so fucked up? Don't you ever think or feel sometimes that we're the fucked up ones?"

"No, not me, bitch. You're crazy. Stop trying to be one of those...What do they call them girls on TV? Oh yeah, the Orange County housewives. Maria, stop trying to be one of those hoes, because you're not them."

"Shay, please. You're tripping. But, like I was saying, fuck him."

Chapter 3

◌

Confessions by Debra Jenkins

DIRECTOR TOM: LaShay, we have no more time to waste. We need you on set now, please.

BILLY: She's on her way, Tom. You don't have to be so rude.

DIRECTOR TOM: I'm not being rude, Billy. But you don't have to be so damn sensitive.

BILLY: Shay's walking up to the front now.

DIRECTOR TOM: LaShay, move over to your left. That's perfect.

DIRECTOR TOM: Everyone, cameras rolling in five, four, three, two. LaShay, we're rolling now.

LASHAY MARIEE: Hello everyone. I'm your host LaShay Mariee. And this is another episode of **Confessions Behind Closed Doors.** *Well, we are going to do something a little different at the show today. Our "confessor" today will be confessing from an undisclosed correctional facility in the United States. When we return, we will all find out who this confessor behind bars is. Don't go anywhere. We'll be right back after these messages.*

DIRECTOR TOM: LaShay, what the hell is wrong with you?

LASHAY MARIEE: What do you mean, Tom? I'm fine.

DIRECTOR TOM: Well, it's not showing on camera, LaShay. You look very tense and angry. Go spruce yourself up a little bit.

LASHAY MARIEE: OK, let me just go to my dressing room. I think I need to go and smoke a cigarette. Where the hell are my cigarettes? Oh, there they are. This shit is getting too stressful for me.

***

"Hey, Maria girl, what are you doing?"

"Nothing, girl. Just sitting here having a drink at that little Tiki Hut you showed me."

"Damn, that sounds nice. I wish I was there. I'm at the set of the show right now though."

"Oh, where are you now? In your dressing room?"

"Yeah, I'm in my dressing room right now. I needed a little break."

"OK, well call me when you get off work. I'm trying to enjoy my margarita."

"OK, bye girl. Love you. Maybe we could hook up and go out after I get off."

"All right. That sounds great. Just call me when you get off. Love you too. Bye-bye."

***

DIRECTOR TOM: Everyone make their way back to the set please. We're on in three minutes.

Come here LaShay. Are you OK now?

LASHAY MARIEE: Yes Tom. I just needed a little bit of time to get myself together. But don't worry. I'm all right now.

DIRECTOR TOM: That's great LaShay. I'm glad to hear that. Well, I want you to open up standing in somewhat of a different area than you would usually. I want you to stand by the doors, so that your shadow is reflecting off the light. Yes, that's great. You look perfect.

OK, everyone, cameras rolling in five, four, three, two. We're rolling now.

LASHAY MARIEE: Hi, everyone and welcome back to the show. Now, before we went to break, we were just about to introduce a special guest and our first "confessor" of this kind ever. Her name is Debra Jenkins. She was a mother, and she was a wife. Now she has no daughter, and her husband is now serving a six-year jail sentence for the murder of… Well, she's here to tell it all. Debra will be here with us through video. Everyone, please welcome Debra Jenkins to the show please.
     [The audience applauds.]

LASHAY MARIEE: Hello, Debra. And how are you today? Debra, are you there? Can you hear me, Debra?

DEBRA: Yeah, I'm here. I'm just listening to you and how you're trying to act like you care. Like you really fucking care. You don't know me to ridicule me; none of you fucking know me to ridicule me.

LASHAY MARIEE: Well, Debra, just so you know, we're not here to ridicule you. I'm just trying to give you a real chance to tell your side of the story to the world. And we're here to listen. So if you do want to, the time is now. But if you don't want to do this, no one's here to force you, Debra. It's your choice. So how about it, Debra? What's going to be your decision? Are you going to confess or choose not to?

DEBRA: Yes, I will choose to confess if everyone will choose to shut up and listen to me for a change.

LASHAY MARIEE: We all are here to listen to you, Debra. Just start whenever you're ready. And take your time.

DEBRA: *Well, what's up, everybody? My name is Debra Jenkins, and I would like to confess something and really get it off my chest for good. It's really been bothering me ever since I got locked up. I don't really know where to begin or where to start.*

LASHAY MARIEE: *Just start wherever you think is the beginning or wherever you feel most comfortable.*

DEBRA: *Well, I haven't really talked about my life or what happened to anybody for a while now. I grew up wanting someone to love me, wanting to feel loved, and would do anything to get that feeling or do anyone. Should I be saying this? Is this played live?*

LASHAY MARIEE: *Debra, I'm not here to judge you. None of us are. We're here to listen to you, and yes, Debra, we are played live. Why do you ask?*

DEBRA: *Oh, I was just curious, that's all. But like I was saying, I was just everywhere with everyone. I just gave up. Something in me just could not keep pushing any longer; I just couldn't take it any fucking more. I began doing heroin—at that time I was only twenty-two.*

LASHAY MARIEE: *Debra, how were you able to deal with that? I mean, you were so young at the time. Knowing that drug is so powerful and addictive, how could you even bare?*

DEBRA: *LaShay, I was so stressed out from how my life was going. I was already on my second miscarriage. By the time I was twenty-three years old I, was looking at eight to ten years for drug trafficking charges. The court had to appoint me a lawyer because, shit, I couldn't afford one. And I had no real family. The lawyer's name was Curtis Jenkins. He really wanted to help me out with my case, and I didn't know why. He knew that I should've gone to jail for what I had done, but I could tell that he really liked me, and I liked him too.*

The entire time the court's judge was telling him to keep secrets from me about the case; he came to tell me everything and then some. He was such a dumb-ass nigga. Maybe if he would've kept me there and did the right thing, none of this shit would've ever happened. Now look at me. I'm in jail all because of that nigga, my daughter is gone, my soul is lost, and I have nothing left to offer myself or the world.

LASHAY MARIEE: Debra do you believe that? Because by you even coming on the show, telling millions of people your story, that shows your courage and that you do have a conscience. Look, Debra, don't feel bad. We are here to listen to you and try to understand your feelings.

DEBRA: Well, Curtis got me free and went against what his boss was telling him to do, which was to leave my black ass in there to rot. But he went against what his boss said and got me the hell out of there. About a week later, he received his release papers. That really made things rough on us. Curtis and I began to date off and on for about twelve months. After that, we finally split and parted ways for about two years. Out of those two years, I had gotten locked up for burglary charges for nine months.

I don't know how in the hell Curtis found out, but he did, and he came to get me out of trouble once again. He bonded me out himself with thirty thousand dollars in cash. After that we decided we were so-called destined to be together. So we moved in to a little sunrise condo in Miami.

The first year we were back together, he fucked me good every night. It was like we were falling in love all over again. We always wanted to be together. I mean, don't get me wrong, we gave each other our space, but when we were together, it was so amazing and beautiful.

In February of 1997, I got pregnant with me and Curtis's first child. It was a girl and we, well his mother, named her Jasmin Jenkins. We loved our daughter. Well, I loved my daughter. He didn't give a fuck about her. Jasmin had the best of everything as a child. Everything was name brand: clothes, shoes, bracelets, and necklaces. You name it, she had it.

When Jasmin turned around the age of eleven or twelve years old, I believe it was, she began to have a very suspicious way about her. My first thought was that maybe she had a little boyfriend, because she had just joined the cheerleading team. She would never tell me, but she had also just begun having her period, so I thought that was also probably the reason of her attitude change. On her thirteenth birthday, I left early that morning to get her present. *[Debra sniffles.]*

LASHAY MARIEE: It's OK, Debra. I know this is hard. Just take your time.

DEBRA: Well, I left early that morning to get her present. She wanted one of those iPod things that play the music and her hair done in freestyle braids. When I came back home, I heard my baby Jasmin crying. So I put down all the bags and walked to her room. On my way doing that, I saw Curtis coming out of her room.

I didn't think anything of it at the time, but he just would not let me into our daughter's room.

He just stood in front of her door and told me to let her have some time to herself. He said that he talked to her already and it was over some boy that had just dumped her the day before her birthday. So I didn't even go in the room. I just listened to him like a dumb ass. I can't believe I didn't even just open the door to check on her.

So the whole day I noticed that Curtis and Jasmin both we're acting very funny. But I didn't see or understand at the time that she was just calling out for my help. About eight days after her birthday—I recall it being around three o'clock in the morning—I felt Curtis get out of our bed. I didn't let him know that I was awake because I had been suspecting he was cheating. When he didn't pick up his phone off of the dresser on the way out the room, I thought he was maybe going to the kitchen to get a midnight snack or something to drink. I just tried to go back to sleep. When he left the room, it was three-oh-five in the morning.

I looked back at the clock when I lightly woke up out of my sleep. He wasn't in the room. The clock then said three-fifty-five. That immediately made me jump out of the bed. First I looked downstairs. The cars were still in the garage, and he wasn't in the kitchen. I just began to wander around the house. I ended up standing in front of my daughter Jasmin's room, looking between the small crack of her door. And what I saw was heart wrenching. It was unspeakable.

LASHAY MARIEE: Debra, what did you see? If I might ask that particular question…

DEBRA: I saw my thirteen-year-old daughter, my baby girl, on her hands and knees, performing oral sex to my husband, her birth father. He had both of his hands clenched around her hair, like she was some hooker off the street that he had just met twenty minutes ago.
    [The audience gasps.]

LASHAY MARIEE: Debra, how did that make you feel, seeing firsthand what was going on? I mean, I know a lot of mothers in the studio audience and our mothers watching at home would feel lost or shocked in some way.
    [The audience applauds.]

DEBRA: To tell you the truth, LaShay, I had not one clue what to do with myself. So I just stood there for about five minutes. That really made me go insane. I mean, I didn't know how to react.

LASHAY MARIEE: So what happened after that, Debra? What was your next move?

DEBRA: I went to the kitchen and grabbed a butcher knife—the biggest one I could find. **[Debra sighs.]** *"I never thought this would be so hard to do for the second time.*

LASHAY MARIEE: I know Debra. Confessing is one of the hardest things you could possibly ever do.

DEBRA: Well, I picked the sharpest knife that we had in the kitchen. And at that time, I didn't have any fucking remorse for Curtis nor my daughter Jasmin. I felt like I was ready to kill the both of them. And I just went at them full force with nothing but rage imbedded in my soul. [Debra bursts into hysterical tears.]

LASHAY MARIEE: Debra, are you OK, honey? Why did you stop?

DEBRA: Look, can you give me one fucking minute, please? I mean, damn. You said I can take my time, right?

LASHAY MARIEE: Yes, Debra, I did say that, and that's what I want you to do—to take your time.

DEBRA: I mean LaShay, I know you can see where I'm going with the whole butcher knife scenario. So that's kind of tough to tell the whole world how screwed up my family really was.

LASHAY MARIEE: Debra, on my notes for you, I saw that you said that you had never admitted to the killing. If so, how did you get convicted of the murder without confessing to the authorities?

DEBRA: Because the evidence was all there. Shit, I was there…my prints on the knife and everything.

LASHAY MARIEE: So, Debra, what happened when you went back into your daughter's room? What exactly did you do?

DEBRA: Well, LaShay, let's just say I wasn't thinking of them as my family or my kin anymore. They were head-on enemies. I went at them like I was taught to do in the streets. First I went for Curtis's triflin' ass. I stabbed him two times in the spine. He's paralyzed from the neck down to this day.

He drug himself out the room as I jumped across the bed directly on to Jasmin. And as I landed on her, so did that massive, thirteen-inch butcher knife I had in my left hand. The knife went straight through the left side of her neck. And all I remember her saying is, "Mommy stop. Please stop." And I just lost it. By the time I was done and the cops had gotten me off of her, she had ninety-eight stab wounds to the face and neck area.

[The audience gasps.]

LASHAY MARIEE: Oh my, Debra. Wait one moment before you continue. I just have one question, and I know many in our audience today probably have the same question. Did you not feel any remorse? I mean, Jasmin was your little baby girl, your first and only child. How could you, or any mother for that matter, do something so brutal?

DEBRA: Well, when I saw that little escapade that was going on behind my back in my house and between my family, that killed me. I felt like after that shit it was just my body and spirit that took over, and they both stole my soul. It was total insanity that I experienced, and I couldn't control it.

SHAY: So, Debra, what happened after that? Were you taken into custody, or was it further investigated?

DEBRA: Yes, yes, it was further investigated. And I was also extradited to an undisclosed correctional facility in the United States.

LASHAY MARIEE: So what exactly happened, Debra? When they did further investigate on your case?

DEBRA: Well, it took them a while to even consider doing an investigation.

LASHAY MARIEE: Why is that, Debra? It sounds like to me that's the first thing that should've been done.

DEBRA: I'll tell you why. First of all, they were so fucking lazy. And second, my prints were on the murder weapon. Plus I was the only one that was not stabbed or assaulted, that was all the investigating they really needed to do. I was in jail for about two years before they decided to reopen the case, to further investigate. This time they said Curtis and I both were on trial together. My lawyer said Curtis's ass sold our house to a silver spoon family, and they found some tapes in the house that they decided to hand over to the authorities.

So the judge said that since the videos were presented, a retrial was demanded in my favor for the insanity plea. When they played the tapes in the courtroom, I expected to see some crazy shit. But not that crazy. I was really in disbelief.

Chapter 4

❧

Back to the Show

DEBRA: The tapes showed Curtis sniffing her panties and jacking off while she danced naked in front of him like a little whore. It was about thirty tapes. The first ten tapes he forced her to have sex with him every day, twice a day. In court, you could see the pattern as they played them one by one. After about the twelfth tape, which meant this was the twelfth day of him doing this shit to my baby girl, my daughter Jasmin started willingly going in our room, performing oral sex on Curtis, and having unprotected sex with him. This might sound crazy, but the whole time the tapes were playing in court, I was looking at her deep in her eyes, and in them I saw enjoyment. It seemed like on that twelfth tape, she knew and liked what they we're doing.

I had no idea about these tapes, and in the courtroom I looked dead into Curtis's eyes and gave off a look so deadly and cursed that he could sense it from across the room. He knew I was pissed off at him for all of this and everything that had happened. Well, at the end of the trial, and it was time for the judge to make her decision, she sentenced Curtis to twenty-five years with the possibility of parole, and she reduced my sentence by two years.

LASHAY MARIEE: Wow! This is one of the craziest confessions we've ever had here—and we've had some crazy ones. So, Debra, how do you feel now that you've finally confessed and gotten your side of the story out there for everyone to know?

DEBRA: I feel great LaShay. I mean, I really do now that someone has let me tell my story without any bullshit. Everyone, thanks for allowing me express something and say how I really have been feeling. Not a lot of people have done that for me in a while, and I just want to say thank you all.

LASHAY MARIEE: Well, Debra, do you think we could open the closed doors so that the world can see who you really are?

DEBRA: Yes LaShay. I'm ready for the world to see. I've waited for this day for a very long time.
[The doors open. Behind them appears a video screen showing Debra sitting in an all-white padded room, wearing an orange jumpsuit, with long black hair tied up in a bun.]

LASHAY MARIEE: Well, everyone, please give it up for Debra Jenkins.
[The audience applauds.]

LASHAY MARIEE: So, Debra, I'm going to get some questions from our studio audience. And we also have some tweets from our Twitter page. Will that be fine, Debra? Do you mind answering some questions today?

DEBRA: No, I don't mind, LaShay. That'll be fine.

LASHAY MARIEE: OK, well, who would like to go first? I know everyone has a question. Hi, ma'am. What's your name and what question do you have for Debra today?

REBECCA: Hi LaShay. My name is Rebecca, and I'm from Florida. I heard your story when it first happened and they were playing it on the news. All I want to say is that, yeah, Curtis was wrong for what he did. But I have a daughter, and I don't think that I would ever do something to her like that.

LASHAY MARIEE: So, Debra, how do you feel about what Rebecca from Florida has to say?

DEBRA: LaShay, I would just say that that's her opinion, and I would say the same thing if I was her.

LASHAY MARIEE: OK, wait one moment, sir, I'm trying to move as fast as I can. You really want to ask this question. It must be a great one.

LAWRENCE: Yes, it is a great one. First off, LaShay, girl you look fabulous darling.

LASHAY MARIEE: Why thank you. You look dashing yourself.

LAWRENCE: My name is Lawrence, but all my friends call me La-La, and I'm from Houston, Texas. I just wanted to say that I hope you die in jail. I don't know how in the hell you only got six years.

LAWRENCE: I'm sorry, Debra, but I have a thirteen-13 year-old sister, and I just feel like if she did stab her daughter ninety-eight times, there was no remorse there. Maybe if it was one or two stab wounds out of pure shock...but it wasn't. It was ninety-eight stab wounds. I feel that the justice system should lock her up and bury her under the jail.

LASHAY MARIEE: OK, well, thank you so much, Lawrence, for expressing your thoughts about this story.

LAWRENCE: No, thank you, LaShay.

DEBRA: Now that everyone else is done talking, can I please say one thing?

LASHAY MARIEE: Yes, Debra of course. What would you like to say?

DEBRA: I just wanted to tell Lawrence, fuck him, and he can go suck his two o'clock dick.

LASHAY MARIEE: Well, this has been another unbelievable episode of **Confessions Behind Closed Doors.** *I'm your host LaShay Mariee. Debra, good luck with everything, and, when you get out, I hope your life is the life you've always wanted. Until next time, everyone. Stay tuned to find out who's our next week's confessor.*

NEXT WEEK ON CONFESSIONS BEHIND CLOSED DOORS...

LASHAY MARIEE: Dominique McCoy, a twenty-eight-year-old Cuban American woman from Miami, Florida, confesses to the world and her missing mother what she had to go through and deal with living with her abusive father and 5 brothers. Tune in next week to hear it all from Dominique McCoy herself.

DIRECTOR TOM: Wow! Fucking ratings are through the roof! LaShay, keep doing what you're doing. I love that participation you're doing with the audience. Keep doing that, and it'll be time to talk about your raise.

LASHAY MARIEE: Look, Tom, I think me and you both know it's been time for my raise.

***

"Hey Maria, girl. What are you doing? Oh, nothing. We're closing down the set now. Did you see the show today? Yes, that shit was crazy. Bitch, why you playing? It was really sad to me. I mean, how could any mother do that to her daughter? Life is crazy, girl, but this show proves that people are crazier. So what are you and your man doing tonight? That's nice. What restaurant are y'all going to? I love that place. Well, have fun, girl. Just call me after and tell me how it went."

Chapter 5

❦

Find Your Own Spotlight!

"Brent, calm down. I had to stay at the office for an extra hour, baby. So I was just supposed to tell my boss 'fuck you,' and just walk out? Well, Brent, honey, it doesn't work like that. But I'll be home in about five minutes. Bye-bye."

Man, I swear all he does is nag, nag, and nag.

***

"Baby, I'm home. Where is everybody?"

"Hey, Mommy! Hey, Mommy, I missed you today."

"Hey, baby, I missed you too. So how was today at school?"

"It was good, but this girl keeps picking on me."

"Well, why is she doing that, Summer?"

"I don't know. I asked what I did to her, and she said that I'm just me."

"Did you tell your teachers about this?"

"Yes, mommy I did, but she just keeps on doing it."

"Well, I will come to your school tomorrow and straighten everything out, baby. Oh, where's your father?"

"In the room getting dressed, waiting for you, Mommy. Where are you and Daddy going tonight?"

"We're going out to eat, honey. And have you done your homework Summer?"

"No, I haven't. I thought that I could wait to do it later."

"Don't give me that lame-ass excuse, Summer. You know you're supposed to start on that as soon as you get home. Now go get to it. Hey, baby!"

"Hey Maria. How was your long day at work?"

"Why did you say it like that?"

"You know why. I made reservations, and we're an hour late, and you still have to get dressed."

"No I don't. I'm just going to wear this."

"No, you're not, Maria. You need to dress casual."

"Yes, I am Brent. So let's just go."

"So should I just take off what I have on then?"

"No, just leave it on, and let's go since we're so late.

OK, Summer, honey, we'll be back later, so finish your homework and then go straight to bed. But first let Miss Sophia check your answers, okay?"

"OK, Mommy. I love you. And you and Daddy have a good time. Bye-bye."

"Bye baby. Now go upstairs and finish doing your homework. Sophia, please make sure she finishes all her work. I know she likes to skip some questions."

"Don't worry about it; I'll take good care of her. You both just go have a nice night."

"OK, thanks Sophia. We'll be back before midnight."

***

"I can't believe we're this late; this is one of the best restaurants in town."

"Brent, please. Let's not fight and bicker while driving. That's how half the accidents happen in this town. We're late. There's nothing we can do about it. So please let's just try and enjoy the rest of our night."

"Well, we can try, but it's not going to be much of a night if our reservations are canceled."

"OK. Whatever. But we're here now, so let's get out of the car and have the best time we can. Let's go. We need to hurry. We can't be another second late. People die for these reservations."

"Hello and welcome to the Silk Lounge. How may I help you today?"

"Well, we actually have reservations under the name of Brent Fernandez."

"Oh. Yes, hello, Mr. Fernandez. We've been waiting for you to arrive for about two hours now. My supervisor did not think you were going to be able to join us tonight, so we gave your table away and canceled your reservations. I'm so sorry, Mr. Fernandez."

"Wow, this is great. This is just classic, Maria."

"OK, thank you. We'll just leave. Bye-bye."

"What do you mean, Brent, by 'this is classic'? I mean, what did you want me to do, lose my job?"

"Look, Maria, I don't know. But you could have done something more than what you did."

***

"Hey, Shay, what's up girl?"

"Nothing much. You sound sad. What happened?"

"Girl, last night was horrible. Everything that could have gone wrong did. I don't know. I just hated it every minute of it."

"Maria, why? What did he do?"

"Well, he was bitching at me ever since I got off of work."

"But why? He doesn't really put in the hours."

"I know. That's the same way I was feeling. But I guess because he had reservations at the Silk Lounge. He's been waiting for a while now to take me."

"That still doesn't give him the right to act like a big prick, Maria."

"I know, Shay. That's basically what I told him, but he didn't want to listen. We've just been so stressed, girl; we haven't really had any time to just focus on us, you know?"

"Girl, I totally understand you. It's the same way with Lamont and I. We never really get to spend any time together. So look, how about you just plan an extravagant trip for you and Brent to get away for a while?

"Girl, I wish. But you know we don't have that kind of money."

"The trip will be on me. I mean, it's the least I could do for you being such a wonderful friend."

"Are you serious, Shay? Please tell me you're serious."

"Yes, crazy I am. I mean, you're my best friend, and I know you love Brent's dumb ass, so go and get your marriage back on track."

"Thanks, girl. I love you so much. I'm going to go start planning it right now. All right and don't hold back. It's wherever you want to go—all expenses paid. And I love you too. Bye-bye."

I hope they work this out; I'm tired of seeing her hurt over this douche bag.

***

"Baby, I'm planning a wonderful trip for us, so start packing."

"What are you talking about, Maria? We don't have the money for taking trips."

"Well, you should be happy that I have such amazing friends."

"What? What are you talking about? Amazing friends? Did one of your friends pay for this amazing trip?"

"Shay. She said that she knows that we've been stressing out lately, and she wanted us to go somewhere and relax."

"Are you fucking serious, Maria? Now you got this bitch giving you money to take trips and bringing me along as your fucking accessory?"

"Brent, what the hell is wrong with you? Shay's doing us this favor out of the kindness of her heart, and you repay her like this?"

"Fuck Shay. This is my family, and we don't need her fucking help. You'd better tell her that. I'll take us on a trip. We don't need her fucking money. Find your own fucking spotlight, Maria. Everywhere Shay goes, you go. If she's at a red-carpet event, you're there right behind her. Even on the set of her show, you're right there on her ass."

"Brent, how dare you say something like that. You're such a fucking pig."

"Look, I don't give a damn. We're not taking her money, and we're not going on that trip, so get over it."

"Wow, you're such an asshole. Bye. I can't be here right now."

"If you go running to your little friend, make sure you tell her what I said."

***

"Hey, are you still working? I need to talk to you."

"No, I'm on break. What's wrong? I thought you would sound a little happier with the trip and everything."

"Well, I was, but you know Brent had to go and mess everything up for me."

"Why, what did he do now, girl?"

"Well, he came in the room while I was planning it, and I told him that you gave us the money to take the trip. Then he just went ballistic. He said that we didn't need your fucking money and we could do it all on our own."

"Girl, he is so fucking crazy. What in the hell is wrong with him?"

"LaShay, we need you back on set now, please."

"Girl, I'm sorry, I have to go back on set. But I promise to call you when I'm done, OK?"

"All right. And in the meantime I'll try to get him to come around."

"You do that. I love you, girl. And don't be down. All men just have big-ass egos. I have to go now, so I love you too. Bye-bye."

Chapter 6

☙☙

Promiscuous

LASHAY MARIEE: Hello, everyone and thank you for joining us on another episode of **Confessions Behind Closed Doors.** *Our confessor today has a very deep confession to share with us all. Her name is Dominique McCoy. Dominique is twenty-eight years old, from Miami, Florida. Please give Dominique a big welcome, everyone.*
    [The audience applauds.]

LASHAY MARIEE: Dominique, how are you doing today?

DOMININQUE McCOY: I'm doing wonderful, LaShay, and I just wanted to say thank you so much for inviting me to the show. I'm ready...ready to tell everyone—mainly my parents—about this and how I feel about it.

LASHAY MARIEE: Well, just hold that thought Dominique. We'll be right back after these messages.

DIRECTOR TOM: OK, everyone, back on set in ten minutes.

***

    "Oh, damn, Brent. You fucking scared me. What are you doing in my dressing room?"
    "Shay, I need to talk to you about something very important."
    "Brent, if this is about you and my girl, Maria, I'm staying out of it."
    "Shay, I'm just here to tell you that I really want you to stay the hell

out of my relationship, and mind your own damn business! I just feel that you're just too fucking nosey for your own good. I mean, we're not all in your business with your fucking man."

"What the hell? Are you fucking serious, Brent?"

"Yes, I am, and don't forget it. Oh yeah, and fuck your trip. We don't need your fucking handout money. We'll pay for our own damn trip, bitch!"

"Security, can you please come assist this lunatic out of my dressing room, please?"

"Don't worry, I'm leaving. But just remember what I said, Shay. Stay the hell out of my relationship!"

***

"Shay, what's going on? Did you call security in?"

"Yes, Billy. Who let him in my dressing room without confirming it with me first?"

"Well, Shay, I knew he was Maria's husband. I didn't think it would be a problem. I'm sorry."

"You could have at least let me know he was in here, Billy!"

"I know, Shay. I'm sorry. I was running back and forth, and it totally slipped my mind."

"That's fine. Just don't let it slip again."

***

DIRECTOR TOM: OK, everyone take their places. And, Billy, please position LaShay on camera three. We're rolling in five, four, three, two. LaShay, you're on now.

LASHAY MARIEE: Hello, everyone, and welcome back to the show. I'm your host LaShay Mariee. And if you're just now tuning in, before we went to break, our first confessor, Dominique McCoy, was just about to tell us her story on how her mom abandoned her when she was only a little girl. She was left with her father and four brothers who later found

*their amusement in abusing her. Dominique, are you ready to confess...
confess to the world, or better yet, yourself?*

*DOMINIQUE MCCOY: Yes LaShay, I am. I really feel like this is the
end. So why hold on to this secret any longer?*

*LASHAY MARIEE: Well, Dominique, just begin whenever you're ready.
Just remember that we are here to listen to you. Take your time.*

DOMINIQUE MCCOY: Well, I really don't know where to begin at.

LASHAY MARIEE: Just start of by telling us all a little bit about yourself.

*DOMINIQUE MCCOY: Well, hello, everyone. My name is Dominique
McCoy. I was born and in Mexico, but was raised in Florida. Growing
up wasn't easy for me, living with my dad and five brothers. Every day
was a challenge for me, in that house every fucking day. When I turned
five, my mom left home with my dentist and never came back—that bitch.
My dad took me and my brothers, and we all moved to a four-bedroom
apartment and sold the house. Six years passed by, and we still had not
heard anything from our mother or where she had gone. It was like she
never existed in our lives.*

*When I turned twelve, my brother, Jordan, who is the second to the
oldest, came into my room, wrapped his hand around me, gripped my
ass, and gave me the first kiss I ever had. We began having sex every
night with one another. The second night he popped my cherry. I must
have bled everywhere. Three years passed, and my body began to change.
My ass got bigger and fuller; I lost all my acne using Proactiv. My hair
grew out. I must say that I looked great at fifteen years old. I soon came
to learn that looking too good was not always good.*

*On July fifteenth, 1997, my dad came into my room while I was
sleeping and started stroking me up and down my thighs. I immediately
jumped up to my feet and asked him what was he doing. And do you
know what this bastard said?*

LASHAY MARIEE: No, Dominique, tell us. What did he say?

Dominique McCoy: He told me to just lay there and pretend that he was my brother Jordan. I could not believe that he had said that. I was in disbelief. I felt very betrayed by my father and Jordan both. He just held me down and fucked me like he didn't know I was his daughter.

LASHAY MARIEE: Dominique that sounds very hard to deal with. How were things after that, Dominique? I mean, I know things were not the same.

Dominique McCoy: They really weren't, LaShay. Things became so out of the ordinary. Even our neighbors could see something was going on. Two years passed by, and my seventeenth birthday was just a week away. My dad still had his perverted ways, and so did my brother Jordan. For my birthday I didn't ask for anything—only to have a party. And I wish I would've never asked for that.

LASHAY MARIEE: Why do you say that, Dominique? I mean, a party sounds like a great way to let off some built-up steam.

Dominique McCoy: When I told my dad about the party, he said sure, but he would put the whole party together for me. He said that I did not have to worry about anything. He said he would even invite everyone and do everything. A week passed by, and my birthday was one day away. I was so excited that I would finally get to have some real fun with my friends.

The whole day of my birthday, I could not feel happy because my lame excuses for brothers were looking at me up and down in a seductive manner. It was really starting to scare me, but I tried to pay them no attention. I continuously asked my dad when my party was going to start. All he told me was just to be patient—everything was under control. By this time it was already eight o'clock at night, and my party was supposed to start four hours earlier. So I knew something was wrong. At nine thirty my dad and all of my brothers came into my room. They all gathered in a circle around my bed.

My youngest brother Justin, the one under me in age, was ten years old at the time. He had this very confused look on his face—like something was about to happen and he wanted nothing to do with it. [Dominique sighs.]

LASHAY MARIEE: Dominique, are you OK? Look, everything will be fine.

Dominique McCoy: LaShay, I'm sorry. I just can't do this. I just can't confess. [Dominique dashes off of the stage.]

LASHAY MARIEE: Dominique, stop! Dominique, come here, please. Dominique! Dominique, why did you run off the stage?

Dominique McCoy: LaShay, I'm not OK. I just can't confess to this. I've already said enough.

LASHAY MARIEE: Dominique, you'll feel so much better if you just come back on stage and reveal who you are.

Dominique McCoy: LaShay, no. I'm telling you I'm done. This is enough!

LASHAY MARIEE: OK, well, thank you so much, Dominique, for coming on the show. And if you do need any kind of counseling, our team here will assist you with that.

Dominique McCoy: Thank you, LaShay. I would really love that. I didn't know it would be this hard to confess.

LASHAY MARIEE: Well, Dominique, we all understand why it was so hard for you to confess. Once again, Dominique thank you so much for coming to the show. I hope everything goes great with your journey in life. Well, everyone, Dominique just could not take it, but I still applaud her for telling as much of her story as she did.

When we return, our next confessor, Jahemerie Dion, will tell us all about his amazing transforming secret on this very stage. Don't go anywhere. We'll be right back with more of **Confessions Behind Closed Doors.** *Stay tuned.*

DIRECTOR TOM: OK, cut. LaShay, that was perfect. OK LaShay our next segment starts in about an hour so, please be ready.

***

YOU'D BETTER
GET
YOURE MAN...

"Hey, girl. What's up?"

"Maria, bitch, don't play with me like you don't know what's going on!"

"Shay, calm down. I really don't know what's going on, so please tell me."

"Your dumb, ignorant-ass man, Brent, came down to my job in a fucking fit of rage and made a big-ass scene. All because I said I would give you that money to go on the trip. What the hell is going on with him?"

"Oh my God, Shay. Are you serious, girl? I'm so sorry."

"Yes, bitch, I'm serious. I'm not lying about it."

"Damn, I said sorry. But you really need to calm the fuck down, because I didn't tell him to go down there to your job."

"Maria, you know what? That's your man, so learn how to tame his ass."

[LaShay hangs up her phone and throws it at the wall.]

"Billy, darling, come into my dressing room, please."

***

"Hey, Shay, what's up? First let me say I'm very sorry for letting him into your dressing room."

"That's OK, Billy. Don't worry about that shit."

"So what's wrong, Shay? Are you doing OK?"

"Well, I just got into it with Maria over Brent coming down here and

acting the way he did."

"Oh, really? And what did she say about it?"

"She said that she didn't know anything about it or what was going on with him being upset about it. Shit, but I did tell her ass to tame her fucking man, and then I just hung up the phone."

"If you want my opinion, Shay. It's really not her fault—especially if he did not even tell her he was coming to your job to confront you about bullshit."

"I know it's not her fault. I was just a little upset at her. Anyway, I can't believe Dominique ran off stage."

"I know. That was crazy. Who would've seen that coming? So aren't you going to change before the next show?"

"How long is it before I have to go back on set?"

"You have about a good thirty minutes before you go on."

"Please go and find Sasha and Chad. Tell them I need them here in my dressing room and that it's almost time for me to go on set."

"I'm going to do that. Just relax and don't worry about Brent. Don't let him come between you and Maria."

"I'm not, Billy. I'm going to call her after the show to apologize."

***

*Joan Davis
Or
Jahemerie Dion.
You Tell Me.*

LASHAY MARIEE: Hello, everyone. I'm your host LaShay Mariee and welcome back to **Confessions Behind Closed Doors.** *Well, I'm going to come and parade through the audience for just a moment. So does anyone in our studio audience have any brief "confessions"? OK, we have a confessor. Wait one moment, sir. Hello and what's your name?*

EDDIE: Hi, LaShay. My name is Eddie Maredo.

LASHAY MARIEE: OK, Eddie, what's your confession for today? And just remember: get straight to the juicy stuff.
    [The audience laughs.]

EDDIE: Well, hi, everyone. My name is Eddie Maredo. And my confession is that when I was younger, around the age of eight, I witnessed my older brother, Roger Maredo; kill a thirteen-year-old little girl named Jessica Jameson. At that time my brother was nineteen, going on twenty years old. I have lived with nightmares every night over that shit.

LASHAY MARIEE: Wow, Eddie. I really don't know what to say, know that's a deep confession. Have the authorities found out about this, and has your brother been charged with the murder?

EDDIE: Well, LaShay, yes the case was just recently opened back up. And my brother is in custody now, waiting his trial.

LASHAY MARIEE: Thank you so much for confessing that with us, Eddie. Is there another confessor in our audience today? Hello, ma'am, and what's your name?

SANDRA: My name is Sandra Harrison, and my confession is that I have a son that is on America's most wanted list for murders in the California area.

LASHAY MARIEE: Sandra, is this really true?

SANDRA: Yes, it is true, LaShay. I'm just tired of being his lay-low creep spot. He has to pay for what he's done.

LASHAY MARIEE: Well, that's some confession, Sandra. Please keep the show updated on everything.
    Wow, these have been some crazy confessions from our studio audience. When we come back from a little break, another confessor will confess right on this very stage. We'll be right back after these messages. Don't go anywhere.

DIRECTOR TOM: Cut. That was amazing, LaShay. Everyone, please be back on set in twenty minutes.

***

"Billy, can you come get me from my dressing room in about five to ten minutes?"

"OK, Shay. Go chill out. I'll come and get you. Oh, and Shay, here are your notes for the next confessor."

"Thanks, Billy. And are these all of the notes?"

"Yes, Shay, that's everything. So just look over them briefly, because they changed the script a little bit."

[LaShay picks up her iPhone to call Lamont]

"Hey, Lamont. It's Shay calling again. I just wanted to say that I'm ready to talk to you, so I guess just call me when you get this message. Bye-bye."

***

DIRECTOR TOM: Cameras rolling In five, four, three, two, one.

LASHAY MARIEE: Hello there. I'm your lovely host LaShay, and welcome back to **Confessions Behind Closed Doors.** *Before we went to break, we were just about to introduce our next confessor, Jahemerie Dion. Jahemerie is here to tell his or her entire life-transforming story: from growing up being bullied, to now being a Brazilian male model. Please welcome Jahemerie Dion to the show.*

[The audience applauds.]

LASHAY MARIEE: Hello, Jahemerie and welcome to the show. Are you ready to confess the truth?

JAHEMERIE: Yes I am, LaShay. I'm just ready to tell the world my story and how I really got to this point in my life.

LASHAY MARIEE: Well, Jahemerie, the floor is yours whenever you would like to begin. And just remember that we're here to listen to you, so take your time. And start whenever you're ready, Jahemerie.

JAHEMERIE: Well, hi, everyone. My name is…Well, my birth name is Joan Davis. Throughout my whole childhood, I was the little, chubby, fat girl who lived around the corner that no one wanted to hang out with. Over the years I went through middle and high school being teased and bullied every day—even my brothers did it.

When I graduated from high school, I had big plans for my life—really big plans—and they didn't include college at all. So I stayed with my mother and father for the next year, planning my escape route. When I turned nineteen, I bought a plane ticket to Brazil. I left my car and all the rest of my belongings at my mother's house, and I just disappeared without telling anyone. I just left. And I honestly had no clue that anyone would even notice chubby me was gone.

LASHAY MARIEE: If I might ask, Jahemerie, why you would say something like that—that no one would notice you were gone?

JAHEMERIE: Well, LaShay, I know that's a little harsh to say, but at that time I weighed about two hundred and fifty pounds, and I looked like shit. I was an outcast—if you want to call it that. After the first week of me being gone, everyone was pitching in to search for me—big fat me that no one would sit with at the lunch table.

LASHAY MARIEE: Well, Jahemerie, how did you find out about all of this? I mean, weren't you on the other side of the world?

JAHEMERIE: Well, believe it or not, they do have a U.S station out there with National U.S news.

LASHAY MARIEE: So, Jahemerie, when you observed that you're missing act really stirred up things within your family and neighborhood, how did that affect you?

JAHEMERIE: LaShay, I felt like I had to get my life together, and every-one, including my parents treated me like an outcast. So at that time I really did not care. I just wanted to start my new life all by myself.

Over the last three years that I've been gone, I've had reconstructive surgeries to reform me into a male—which I am today.

[**The audience gasps.**]

JAHEMERIE: Yes, I know that's crazy, but I'm going to go back home with my new and improved persona. I know that I'm going to have to face a lot of upset people—and also my family members—very soon.

LASHAY MARIEE: So how do you feel about having to make that step, Jahemerie? How do you feel about all the people you might have upset these last couple of years?

JAHEMERIE: LaShay, like I said before, I feel like they didn't care or show me they cared, so I had to show them I could have the same atti-tude—the same noncaring, hatred attitude they dished off to me.

LASHAY MARIEE: Well, thank you so much, Jahemerie, for coming to the show and sharing your confession with us. I hope everything goes great with you and your situation.

JAHEMERIE: Thank you so much LaShay, for allowing me this opportunity.

LASHAY MARIEE: So, Jahemerie, are you ready to come from behind those closed doors and show the world the new and transformed you? Are you ready to put the face with your confession?

JAHEMERIE: LaShay, I am more than ready. It's past due. Please open the doors.

[**The doors open. Out steps twenty-three-year-old Jahemerie Dion, with long black wavy hair drop dead gorgeous who is six feet tall with caramel skin, looking like a Brazilian male model. The audience applauds**]

LASHAY MARIEE: Calm down, ladies. Jahemerie, you're going to have to go back behind those closed doors! You have all the ladies in our studio audience going crazy. Wow, you look amazing—and I do mean amazing. I'm sure a lot of ladies in the audience today would love to know are you single.

JAHEMERIE: Yes, LaShay, I am single, but I don't know why, because I'm looking.

LASHAY MARIEE: Well, I'm sure you're going to find your soul mate soon. Who knows? She might be in this audience today!
    *[*The women in the audience applaud.*]*

JAHEMERIE: I hope so, LaShay. I really do hope so. That would make me so happy.

LASHAY MARIEE: Well, once again, Jahemerie, thank you so much for coming to the show and sharing your story with us. I know everyone at the show, including our audience, would love for you to keep us updated with how your life is going.

JAHEMERIE: Of course, LaShay. I would love to keep in touch with the show, and if it's not a problem, in touch with you too.
    *[*The audience applauds.*]*

LASHAY MARIEE: That's so kind of you, Jahemerie. I would love for you to keep me and the show updated.

JAHEMERIE: Thank you all so much for allowing me to get this out to the world and my message, which is: Live your life. Before you leave this world, improve yourself from the inside out, the way that fits you best.

LASHAY MARIEE: This has been another episode of **Confessions Behind Closed Doors.** *Thank you all so much for tuning in with us today. I'm your host LaShay Mariee. Thank you and good night.*

NEXT WEEK ON CONFESSIONS BEHIND CLOSED DOORS...

LASHAY MARIEE: See where a life of partying and selling drugs, plus sleeping with multiple women, leads Michael Johnson, a thug from the Bronx of New York.

Chapter 7

❧

My Journal

"Hey, Lamont. It's Shay again. I was just calling because you haven't returned any of my calls. I might be going on a little vacation, and I just wanted to know if you would want to accompany me? I'm willing to forgive you for the other night and start all over again. So when you get this message, please call me back. I love you, baby. Bye-bye."

***

MY JOURNAL

Dear Journal:

I don't know what to do anymore. Lamont isn't calling me back. I'm going insane. I feel so desperate, continuously calling him and leaving messages on his voice mail. I'm starting to wonder: should I just venture off like it appears he is, or should I just wait for him and be depressed forever? I'm confused only because I really love him, not because I can't live without him.

Signed: A Confused Woman

***

"Hey, Maria, girl. What are you doing?"
"Nothing, bitch. Have you calmed down yet?"
"Yes, I have, and that's why I'm calling: to say that I apologize, and it really was not your fault that Brent came down to my job and acted that way."

"Well, thanks for apologizing, girl. I forgive you. Oh, and I talked to Brent. He said that he wants to apologize to you."

"There's no need for that. Just tell him that we're cool with each other and to just not do that anymore. So, anyways, change of subject. What are you doing for the rest of the day?"

"Right now I'm still at work, and my fucking boss, Terrie, is pissing me off."

"Well, what time do you get off of work?"

"I'm not really sure, but I'm thinking at around ten o'clock tonight."

"OK. Well, call me after you get off. Maybe we can go have some drinks at that winery down the street from my house—you know, if your man Brent is OK with that."

"Bitch, I'm not a child, and Brent damn sure isn't my missing father. Of course I can chill with you."

"OK, we'll see. Just call me when you get off work girl. And, Maria, thanks for being my friend."

"No problem, girl. You know we're friends for life."

***

MY JOURNAL

Dear Journal:

I feel so much happier now that I've talked to Maria about everything. She's my best friend, and I never want to lose her friendship over something so petty. She said Brent apologized, but deep down inside, I think she's doing it for him, and I'm just going to go along with it. I just don't want to lose her as a friend over such a jerk of a man.

Signed: What's a Best Friend to
Do When She's
Done Everything?

***

"Dad, I just don't understand Mom. Why is she acting like that? I'm just trying to help, and all she can do is deny me."

"Honey, just calm down. This is your father you're talking to."

"I'm sorry, Dad. I'm just so upset. I came all the way out here as soon as I heard you guys weren't doing good, and she's just pushing me away."

"I know, baby, but that's your mom, and you have to understand that you put your mother and I through a lot of bullshit, LaShay. You just have to understand that your mom doesn't like handouts from anyone."

"Dad, you can't be serious. I'm your daughter. You and Mom raised me and gave me everything I needed and wanted. So why can't I help the both of you? Man, Mom is tripping—she really is."

"Ah, LaShay, watch your mouth in my house. When you're here, show some damn respect!"

"Yes, sir. I'm sorry, Dad. But, anyways, I'm going to Barbados. So I'll just leave this money with you then. Tell Mom I love her. OK, Dad?"

"OK. And, LaShay sweetie, she'll come around. Just give her some time, baby girl."

"Thanks, Dad. I'll call you guys when I land. I love you."

"OK, sweetie. You make sure you call. And I love you too."

***

"Hey, Maria. What's up, girl?"

"Nothing much. Just getting off from work. Where are you at right now?"

"At the airport. I just left my parents' house."

"So how did everything go with your mom? Was she glad to see you, or was she upset as always?"

"She was OK. But she still won't accept anything from me, and I'm getting so frustrated with her."

"What did you try to give her this time?"

"Well, I tried to give her some money for her and my dad. But she wouldn't take it, and that is really pissing me off."

"So how are you feeling about that? You can tell me. I'll listen."

"I'm not really trying to talk about it too much. I refuse to feel angry

while I'm in beautiful Barbados. I will call you when I land. I need this vacation—I'm so stressed."

"OK. Just call me when you get situated. Bye, girl."

***

MY JOURNAL

Dear Journal:

I'm on the plane, just taking in everything that's going on with me in my life. Hopefully going on this trip will help me out and relax me a little bit. I feel like I can't win no matter how known I am. I mean, why does my mother have to be in such denial? I love her, and I just feel like she should not have to want for anything now that I'm in the position to do it for her. I want to be there for my mother and my father both. But how can I when they both—well, when my mother won't let me. What am I to do when I've done all that I can?

Signed: What's a Girl to Do When She's Done Everything?

***

"Hey, honey, did LaShay leave already?"

"Yes, she did. Why would you act that way, Diana? She's your daughter."

"Well, Fred, I just can't cope with how a lot of things are going."

"Diana, you're just jealous of your own daughter, and that's not right. She's trying to help us, her parents."

"Fred, what the hell do you mean—jealous of my daughter? Are you serious?"

"OK, whatever Diana. I'm sorry. Well, she's gone. But she did say that she would call when she landed. Would you like to talk to her when she calls?"

"Yes, honey, I would love to talk to her. That would be great."

64

"Wonderful first step, dear. She's really going to enjoy hearing from you."

"Do you really think so, Fred? I mean, I know that I've been pretty harsh toward the both of you lately, and I'm sorry, honey. I really am. Will you forgive me?"

"Of course, baby. I love you so much, and I will always be here for you, Diana."

***

"Hi, Dad. I just landed. How is everything with Mom?"

"Oh, she's fine, but she wants to talk to you."

"Really, Dad? How do you know?"

"Well, because we talked for a while and concluded it's not worth losing the family over. I'm going to put your mother on the phone now, OK, baby doll?"

"OK, Dad. Thanks for talking to her."

"No problem, honey. I'm handing her the phone now. Bye-bye."

"Hello. Hi, Mom. How's everything going?"

"I'm fine, dear. How's everything going with you?"

"Oh, everything's been fine, Mom; my schedule has just been very crazy."

"Look, I just wanted to say that I apologize for the way I behaved earlier."

"Thanks, Mom. I'm sorry too for trying to offer you something in that way. But I just don't want you or Dad to want for anything."

"LaShay, we are your parents, and we don't always need your help, sweetie. We can take care of ourselves."

"Well, yeah, let's change the subject, Mom."

"What did you say, LaShay? What did you just mumble?"

"Nothing, Mother. Forget about it. But I really wanted you and Dad to come with me."

"Well, baby, your father and I have things we have to take care of out here."

"Like what, Mom? I gave Dad the money on the card."

"You did what? He did not tell me anything about that."

"Mom, calm down. I left it there. I forced him to take it because you wouldn't."

"LaShay, girl, you'd better watch the way you're talking to me."

"Sorry, Mom. But why can't you just accept this one thing from me? Just this one thing?"

"I can, LaShay. I will accept it. So how much did you put on the card?"

"Mom, I really don't remember, but it will be enough. I mean atleast enough to catch up on you guys bills. Well, I love you, Mom. I'm going to go on the beach for a little while."

"OK, I love you too, baby. Have fun. And, LaShay, baby?"

"I love you too, Mother. What is it?"

"Just wanted to say thank you for the money and for helping your father and I in our times of need. Bye-bye."

***

MY JOURNAL

Dear Journal:

My trip to Barbados is starting off wonderfully. I talked to my mother, and she apologized to me. To me! I can't believe it. We talked for about an hour—all the way from the airport to the drive to my cabin. I feel like we really bonded, and I love that. Oh, and she accepted the money that I gave her and my father. On the phone she asked me how much did I put on the card? I told her enough to catch up on all of their bills. I put a little over two million on that card. I just want them to be OK, and I want them to see how much I appreciate them.

It's so beautiful out here and so serene. It seems like a lot of things are coming out great and in my favor. If Lamont gets his shit together, then everything will be wonderful. But life is never too perfect. Or is it?

Signed: I'm Searching for Perfection. Can I Get It?

***

66

"Thomas, is that you? Hey, Thomas!"

"Excuse me. Do I know you?"

"Well, I know I have on face cream, but I didn't think I would look that different. It's me: LaShayMariee from high school."

"Oh, hi, LaShay! Give me a hug, girl. You look amazing."

"Whatever, Thomas. But you don't look too bad yourself."

"So I know you've been doing wonderful, career-wise and everything in between. I see you every time I turn on my TV or get on the Internet."

"Well, you know I try my best. So what about you, Mr. Thomas? What do you do now?"

"Well, Miss LaShay, if you must know, I'm a doctor now."

"Really? I never thought of you as the doctor type of guy."

"Well, now I am the doctor type of guy. I stopped all that nonsense I was doing. I buckled down, went to school, and graduated with a 4.0 grade point average at the top of my class. Then I transferred to Harvard."

"OK, Thomas. That's wonderful. I'm so proud of you. So are you married, Dr. Thomas?"

"Why do you ask that, LaShay? Is there a ring on my finger? I don't have a ring on, so that means I'm not married, LaShay. I got engaged last year to a woman who I thought I was destined to be with, but to her it was just a little fling."

"So why couldn't you both make it work out? I mean, you were engaged to each other, not just boyfriend and girlfriend."

"Well, she ran off with my brother and half my bank account and our two sons. I don't know where the hell she's at. I haven't heard from her in over a year."

"Oh my God. I'm so sorry, Thomas. I'm really sorry to hear that."

"Yeah, LaShay, I bet you think that's such a great confession, don't you?"

"Thomas, what do you mean? It's not like that. I don't bring my work on vacation with me, Thomas."

"I'm sorry, LaShay. It's just that a lot of my feelings are starting to come back for you. I really didn't expect to see you here, but I'm glad I did. So are you still seeing that guy Lamont?"

"Yes, we're still together, but lately we've been having problems. It's stressful having the press and media taking pictures of our every move. So right now he's not picking the phone up for me. He hasn't been for two weeks."

"Well, just relax here and enjoy beautiful Barbados. I'm here to forget about everything also. I'm on vacation, and no one is to call me Dr. Thomas Vendell. It's just Thomas."

"I know. I feel the same way. So what are you about to get into?"

"Ugh! Nothing much. I'll probably go change and grab a drink at the SHAK...I think that's what they call it? Would you like to meet back up here and go together...unless you have some business to tend to?"

"Thomas, shut up. Of course I would love to. Let's meet back here at four o'clock. What time it is now?"

"It's three fifteen. So I'll see you at four o'clock, OK, sweetie?"

"OK, Thomas, see you later. I'm going to go and get ready."

***

MY JOURNAL

Dear Journal:

My day is just getting better and better. I ran into my old childhood friend and boyfriend, Thomas Vendell. He's a graduate from Harvard, and he's a doctor now. It was so refreshing to see him. He looked wonderful from head to toe, his smile down to his feet—which I saw through his Gucci sandals from last season, but that's fine. We are meeting up in about an hour for drinks at this little bar called the SHAK.

Am I falling in love? I'm already involved in a dedicated relationship, but Lamont still hasn't called me, and it's going on three weeks now. I'm starting to get scared. I don't know what to do anymore. He's leaving me in suspense, and that's not right. I'm too turned on by Thomas and have too much history with him to have drinks with him in Barbados to let nothing happen. But if my man can't return any of my phone calls, why shouldn't I go have drinks with Thomas and whatever happens just happens?

Signed: Whatever Happens, Happens

***

"Hi, LaShay. I didn't think you were going to show up."
"Well, you know I thought it over for a while and decided to come."
"I kind of figured that out; you're thirty-five minutes late."
"Fashionably late—and never ever forget."
"Wow, LaShay, you've really turned Hollywood."
"Thomas, I'm just joking around, and I see that you have that stuck-up Harvardish attitude."
"OK, OK, LaShay. Let's not start off on the wrong foot with one another."
"I'm sorry. You look very sexy this evening. So are you ready to have a couple of drinks?"
"I sure am now. Let's go!"

***

[Five hours, three margaritas three vodka shots, nine Patron shots, and four strawberry daiquiris later.]
Would you like to dance, LaShay?"
"I can barely stand up, Thomas. How am I going to dance?"
"Well, that's fine. I'll hold you up."
"Thomas, I can't feel my legs right now."
"I hope he doesn't see my knees buckling."
"LaShay, are you OK? You can barely stand."
"Oh my God he smells so damn good. I have to get the hell out of here."
"Yes, Thomas, I'm fine. I think I should go lie down in my room. I'm not feeling too good right now."

"What's wrong? Do you want me to walk you to your room? It will be no problem...no problem at all."

"I'm just a little sick from the alcohol, but I'll be fine. I will walk myself back to my room. Thanks anyway."

"LaShay, you're crazy, but I'm walking you back; I don't want anything to happen to you. That would really break my heart."

"Well, come on and walk me, but you'd better not try no any funny shit."

"Of course. Why would you think something like that, LaShay? I mean, do you really think that little of me?"

"No, I don't Thomas. But we have been drinking a lot, and people try things when they're under the influence."

"OK, LaShay. Don't be so paranoid. I promise I won't try anything. So where is your room at? Somewhere fancy I know?"

"It's just down the road here."

"Oh, I thought you were at the Marriot in some high-end suite."

"No, I suppose I downgraded for the weekend. I didn't want to be around a lot of people, so I just decided to rent out this cabin for a week or so. Well, here we are."

"This is a huge cabin. I've never seen this here before."

"Yes, here we are. So I guess this would be good night, Thomas."

"Yes, LaShay, unfortunately it is going to be good night. You know, LaShay, it doesn't have to be good night; it could be good morning."

"No, Thomas, I don't think so. It's good night tonight."

"OK, good night LaShay, and I sure hope to see you tomorrow."

***

"Hey, Lamont, this is LaShay again. Have you forgotten we're supposed to be together? Did you send out some kind of break-up memo that I did not receive on my end and got delayed to my phone? Look, if you don't call me by tomorrow night, we are really completely over! I'm in beautiful Barbados with men jumping at me. Get your shit together, and do it fast."

***

Chapter 7

MY JOURNAL

Dear Journal:

I'm so drunk right now I don't know what to do. I had a great time with Mr. Thomas Vendell. He showed me a wonderful time—I loved it. We danced, talked, laughed, drank. It was just so relaxing being with him. He tried to come in my room with me, but I wasn't having that shit—at least not yet. But I had so much fun with him. He kind of made me forget about Lamont in a way—but not completely. That's why he didn't get in the room.

Lamont still is not picking up the phone for me. I left him a message, telling him to get his shit together and get it together fast! I mean, shit, I'm in Barbados by myself, and you can't pick up your phone for me? That is bullshit. So if he does not call me by tomorrow night, I'm telling Thomas to walk me back to my room again—and this time I'm letting him in.

Signed: Am I Being Too Desperate?

***

"Good morning. I didn't think you were coming to town for breakfast this morning."

"Why do you say that?"

"You were so toasted last night."

"Well, that was just something I needed to do. I'm always so closed in because of my career."

"Well, with me you would never have to feel closed in."

"Let's CTS, Thomas. So what are you going to eat for breakfast?"

"Do you really still do that high school stuff you and your little group of chicken-head friends use to do? All that CTS—Change the Subject? And that GOMF—Get Out My Face—secret word type of shit?"

"Yes, I do, and I still have some of those chicken-head friends you're talking about."

"Sorry. I guess that's a bit of a sore subject. So let's just CTS. I don't know what I want to eat. Maybe a little bit of everything…including you, LaShay."

"Thomas, get over yourself, please. You're so silly."

"Would you like for me to fix your plate, LaShay?"

"Yeah, sure. Thanks a lot, Thomas. That's so sweet."

"What would you like to eat? They have everything up there."

"I don't know—just surprise me."

***

MY JOURNAL

Dear Journal:

I'm eating breakfast with Thomas this morning; he just went to fix my plate. It's going great. This is so amazing. Oh, and Lamont still has until tonight to call me, or I'm going at Thomas full force.

Signed: I'm A Full-Force Kind of Girl

***

"Oh my god LaShay! Do you really still write in those damn journals every damn day? Girl, you haven't changed one bit, have you?"

"No, Thomas, I haven't changed one bit. I love my journals; they keep me sane. So what about you, do you still have your Snugga Puss?"

"I loved that stuffed animal, but, no, I don't still have Mr. Snugga Puss. I got rid of him my first year of Harvard."

"Wow, that was very Harvardish of you. So how do you like the food here? You put a lot of bacon on my plate."

"Because you lost a lot of weight. And if we're going to be together, I want you back thick like the old LaShay on the block I knew."

Chapter 8

☙❧

Still No Call

"Lamont, it's over! I'm tired of calling and calling you just to get your voice mail. Don't worry about me calling and calling you anymore. I don't care if the press finds out. I don't care what the media says. It's totally over between us. We're done."

***

"Hey, Maria, it's Shay. Call me when you get this message, girl. I just broke up with Lamont. Well, he hasn't been picking up the phone for me, so I think he's doing all the breaking up. Call me, girl, ASAP, when you get this message. I really need my best friend to give me some advice."

[Thomas knocks on LaShay's door]
"Wait just one moment please, Thomas." OK, get yourself together, Shay. You're not in a relationship anymore. Don't mess this up. *"Hi, Thomas. You clean up very nice."*

"I try. And what about you, LaShay? You're still in your pajamas. It's midday. What's wrong?"

"Well, Thomas, I just broke up with my boyfriend through voice mail, so I'm feeling a little down right now."

"Don't feel that way, LaShay. You're too beautiful and too smart. And you have too much of a heart to be dealing with such a big chump like Lamont."

[LaShay giggles.]

"See? Now that's what I like to see—your beautiful smile. Get dressed and dazzled up. Let me take you out for a night on the town. I'll be back in an hour to get you. Is it a date?"

"Yes, Thomas, it's a date."

***

[LaShay's phone rings, with Lamont's name on the front screen]

"So now you're trying to call me? Are you serious? I don't even think so, Lamont. It's over!"

"Shay, baby, I've been out of town."

"So that means you can't pick up the phone for me? You haven't called me or answered any of my calls for the last three weeks."

"Shay, calm down. I was thinking about you the whole time I was there."

"Lamont, I don't care what you're saying. We're over, and that's that. Plus, someone has already stepped up their shit. So bye, Lamont."

"Shay, Shay, baby! Please don't hang up the phone. I'm sorry. Damn, she hung up!"

***

"Lamont, baby, don't worry about her. We're in beautiful Hawaii, having a great time. Let's continue doing so."

"Maria, shut the hell up. That's my girl and your best friend. You're so damn selfish!"

"Lamont, what do you mean I'm selfish? That's your girl. You're not so damn innocent yourself."

"I know, I know. We both know that this shit is wrong, Maria. I have to go to Barbados and get Shay. I'm trying to marry her, Maria. You know that!"

"So you mean to tell me what we have is just over, Lamont?"

"Maria, we didn't have anything—just a couple of nights in the room. And, shit, you got paid…paid to keep your mouth closed. I have to go to Barbados and get Shay. Bye."

"Lamont don't go. Baby, don't go!"

[Lamont slams the room door, leaving Maria alone.]

Why does that bitch get everything all the time? This isn't over. He has no idea this isn't over.

***

"Come in, the door is open."

"Hey, LaShay, you know, you really shouldn't leave your door unlocked like that."

"Oh, thanks. I'll make sure not to do that again. I don't want to be assassinated, especially in Barbados."

"So what did you have in mind for us to do this evening?"

"I was thinking we could just chill out here in my room for a while."

"LaShay, if you don't mind me saying…A fish out of water will never live too long."

"So, Thomas, if I might ask…What do you mean by that? Because I literally have no clue."

"Well, LaShay, all I'm saying is, keep your eyes open. You'll never know when Cupid is hitting you with that damn arrow."

"If I'm catching what you're saying, Thomas, I would think you're trying to make a pass at me."

"You would be somewhat correct about that, LaShay. Actually, you are correct. But I would want us to take things slow—but not too slow. So how do you feel about everything that's going on with you and your man?"

"First of all, Thomas, that's none of your business. And second of all, he's no longer my man. I told you it's over between him and i completely."

"I'm so sorry to hear that, LaShay. Are you OK?"

[He really means that he's excited to hear that.].

"Thanks, Thomas, but I'm OK. I'll be fine."

"How can I take your mind off of all that?"

"Well, you can start by giving me a hug. Oh, I'm sorry, Thomas. Wait one moment. I need to answer the phone. It might be important."

***

"Hey, Shay. It's Maria, girl. I got your message. Is everything OK with you and Lamont?"

"Girl, he and I are over. I've been trying to get in touch with him for about three weeks now. I mean it girl. This time he and I are done! He called me though, earlier today."

"Oh, for real? And what did he say?"

"He said that he's just been busy doing business. Girl, I told him there isn't that much business in the world, and then I hung up the phone. Like I told him, I'm not about to keep dealing with his bullshit. So why haven't you been picking up your phone for me lately?"

"Oh, I've just been going through the same shit with Brent's ass. Is everything going OK with you in Barbados?"

"It's going great, but do you remember Thomas Vendell from middle and high school?"

"Who are you talking about? Sexy Thomas that you hooked up with in high school?"

""Yes, that Thomas. I ran into him down here in Barbados on the way to check in my room. He's a doctor now."

"Wow, that's great. He really changed his life around."

"Yes, he did. Well, Maria, I have to go know now. I'll call you back when I'm done."

"When you're done doing what?"

"When I'm done entertaining my guest. I invited Thomas back to my room—but just to watch some movies and eat some popcorn."

"That's such bullshit, Shay."

"Maria, bye. I have to go. I'll call you with an update on what's going on."

"OK, bye, girl. Call me later."

So this is what Lamont is running to Barbados for. Well, he's going to get what he's looking for.

***

"I'm so sorry about that, Thomas. That was my BFF. She just wanted to know if I was OK."

"That's OK LaShay. Trust me. I understand women and their gossip spurts. When you feel the urge, you have to go for it. So was she—or did she—sound a little hurt about everything?"

"Why would she be hurt? I'm in a relationship with Lamont, not her."

"No, LaShay, I'm just saying that you did state that the both of you were best friends—you know, BFFs—so I thought she was just feeling a little pain for you, that's all. So anyways, would you like to go on the beach ledge?"

"It's dark outside, Thomas. We won't be able to see anything!"

"Are you insane? The ledge is always lit up at night. Come on. You already look beautiful. You don't need any makeup on. Let's go."

"Thomas, if it ever came down to it would you protect me from anything? Like a precious diamond?"

"You shouldn't even ask me that. I've always loved you girl."

"Let's go then. I can't wait to see the stars."

***

"It's so beautiful out here. I never want to go back home."

"I feel the same way every time I come out here."

"Oh, you've been here more than once?"

"Yes, I've been here on about twenty to thirty different occasions."

"Wow. Well, I can see why. It is so gorgeous here; they do really light the ledge up at night."

"I told you, you would love it, LaShay. It's beautiful out here—just like you. I fell in love with it the first time I came here. And, LaShay, I'm talking about you and the ledge—but especially you."

"Do you really feel that way, Thomas?"

"Yes, LaShay, I do. I have always had feelings for you. You know that. Even after you left me to go after your dreams, I never stopped caring for you, but you stopped writing. So what about you? Did you stop caring for me, LaShay? And please don't lie."

"Thomas, I can't lie. I did think about you from time to time, but I was focused on my career and relationship at that time. You know a couple years after we stopped talking, I met Lamont."

"I understand, LaShay. You had moved on. Trust me, I understand that."

"Thomas, please shut up. You have no room to talk. You were engaged and on the verge of getting married. So you should have nothing to say. Look, we both had our own separate lives, Thomas, that we can't blame one another for. OK?

"You're right, LaShay."

"Well, we finally made It all the way up. It's even more beautiful at the top of the ledge."

"Yes, you are more beautiful up here. Can I have a kiss, LaShay? I know you just broke up with your man, but I thought I still might ask. Can I be the one to comfort you?"

"Shut up and just kiss me already, Thomas. I thought you would never ask.

[Thomas grips LaShay's ass tightly and strokes her up and down.]

"No!"

"LaShay, what's wrong? What did I do wrong?"

"We're moving way too fast, Thomas; we need to slow everything down. I'm going to take a walk down the ledge, I'll be right back."

"Well, LaShay let me come with you."

"Thomas, just wait here. I'll be right back; I really just want to go alone, OK Thomas?"

"OK, LaShay. I'll be waiting for you. Don't take too long, or I'm coming down there to get you."

Chapter 9

ॐ

Over the Edge

MY THOUGHTS:
PART ONE

That felt so amazing, Shay. Why did you leave? You need to get your ass back up there. Better yet, you need to take him back to your cabin and ride him like the bad boy he really is.

But if I do, he's going to think I'm moving too fast. Then he'll shy away from me.

Girl, fuck that. You're in Barbados. That's what he expects you to act like.

I'm so pissed off at Lamont, but I do still miss him a lot.

Girl, what are you still thinking of him for? You've been hearing nothing but voice mail for the past three weeks.

I'm so confused. I wonder if I should just go back to my cabin and leave Thomas here on the ledge alone.

***

"Lamont! What are you doing here? How did you get here?"

"Don't Lamont me. I just saw you tongue choke that guy, Shay."

"Lamont, stop. Don't go up there bothering him. You and I are over; you know that. So why are you down here fucking up my trip?"

"I knew you were down here fucking around, Shay. You not nothing but a Hollywood hoe!"

"Lamont, you know what? Go to hell, and please just get out of my life."

"Yes, I'll do that gladly—just after I confront this weak-ass nigga."

"Lamont, stop. Don't go up there. Just leave."

***

"Who are you, man?"

"Excuse me, what the hell are you doing? Who are you?"

"Thomas, Thomas, I'm so sorry about this. I tried to stop him. I'm so sorry. Lamont, please just leave; don't do this. We are over!"

"So, Thomas, why in the hell are you up here kissing and pressing all on my bitch?"

"Man, Lamont, we're two grown men here. LaShay is a grown and very independent woman. She can make her own decisions. From what I've been told, you both are over and done with."

"No, that was false information, brother. Shay's my girl. That's how it's always been, and that's how it's going to stay."

"Lamont, you have no right…no right at all to do what you're trying to do. The only time you called me is when I left that voice mail on your phone telling you I was moving on."

"Man, you really just need to get out of here. You're making a ruckus, and it's uncalled-for."

"Like I said before: stay the hell out of our relationship. Keep talking. Just keep talking, and watch me come over there and handle you, pretty boy Thomas."

"Let's not get ahead of ourselves, Mr. Businessman of the Year."

"Yeah, and don't you forget it!"

"Look, Lamont, this is over. Stop making a scene, and please just leave."

"It's not that easy, Shay. You think you can just break up with me. I'm Lamont Jackson. I'm worth two-point-five billion dollars."

"That's where you go wrong. Because that's all your worth is: money—nothing else. I desire a real, honest, and true man. You've showed me that you can't come close to being the man I want. Screw your bank account. I have my own." "Thomas, watch out! Lamont stop! Don't push him! Thomas! Thomas!"

[Thomas is pushed over the ledge, by Lamont]

"Oh my God, Lamont! What the hell is wrong with you? I'm going to find help. You're insane! Lamont, let go of my arm now, and I mean, it!"

"I'm not letting you go anywhere. We are in this together. We both pushed him, the way I see it. Or you pushed him all by yourself—depending on how much I'm willing to spend. So which one do you choose, Shay? I'm being quite generous here."

"Lamont, you're crazy! Let me go now!"

"Look, Shay, let's just go home and act like nothing ever happened, OK? Do you hear me? I mean, it, Shay. Let's just keep our mouths closed about this. Where are you going, Shay? Are you serious? Don't walk away from me."

"I'm going to my cabin; I need to get the hell away from you."

"Shay, baby, I'm sorry. I really am. But you honestly don't think I was going to let him go so he could fuck up my career."

"Lamont, are you fucking serious? Listen to yourself. You didn't punch him or rough him up a little bit. You pushed him over the fucking ledge. You pushed him over the high ledge to die."

"If you say that any louder, the cops will hear you. Calm down, Shay."

"Or what, Lamont? Are you going to kill me too? Is that your solution to everything?"

"Shay, just don't forget that we both pushed him—you and I together."

"Lamont, you wish it happened that way. Goodbye."

"I already told you I'm coming with you to your room."

"No, you're not. Stay away from me, Lamont."

***

MY THOUGHTS:
PART TWO

Lamont looks so damn good standing in front of me right now.
    Girl, snap out of it! He just killed Thomas.

But it just made me so wet for some reason. Shit, am I wrong for thinking that?

***

"Shay, so can I come with you to the room, baby?"

"Lamont, no. This is crazy. You're crazy if you think I'm going to let you—a killer—come in my room with me. I don't think so."

"Shay, you know that was an accident. I would have never pushed him if your tongue wasn't all down his throat."

"So you just kill him, Lamont, because I kissed him? Bye, Lamont. It's over. Please just leave." [Shay slams her cabin door in a rage over what just happened.]

"Shay, open the door. Look, baby, I'm sorry. Please just open the damn door!"

***

"Hey, Maria. Look, I need you to do something for me."

"Baby, where have you been? You haven't called me in hours. I've been worried about you, boo."

"Maria, it's not time for all of that right now. I need for you to call Shay and ask her what's going on between me and her. If she seems mad, like I know she's going to be, just try to get me back on her good side."

"Lamont, fuck that. I will not do that fake-ass bullshit. We were just fucking, Lamont. I'm in love with you. So why in the hell would I call and basically beg her to get back with you?"

"Maria, look, you'd better get your shit together. This is my life you're fucking with. If you want me to keep helping you out financially, you'd better change your fucking attitude."

"So what do you want me to tell her, daddy?"

"That's more like it. But I don't know what you should say. She's your best friend. You'll know what to say before I do. Just tell her some shit—like she knows I'm the one for her and she knows that she would never find anyone like me again."

"Oh, and baby? I need about four stacks for this new purse I want."

"Bitch, I just spent forty thousand dollars on your ass. Back the fuck up out of my wallet. You are not my girl. Make sure you do what I said and call her. Bye. I have to go now."

Chapter 10

❧

Lamont and Maria

I really don't want to call this bitch. Lamont is really tripping.
"Hello? Can you hear me, Shay?"

"Yeah. Hey, Maria girl, what's up?"

"Nothing, girl. I was trying to call you and see how you were doing."

"Oh, I'm doing much better from earlier. I'm just over and done with him."

"Girl, that's good. You're too good for him, Shay. He does not deserve a strong woman like you, girl."

"Thanks, Maria. You're always here for me."

"Friends to the end, girl. You know that. Well, I'm going to let you get some sleep, OK?"

"OK, girl. I'll call you if something else crazy happens. Bye-bye."

Finally, Lamont is going to be all mines—just like I planned.

***

"Hey, boo, I did what you told me to do. Are you happy now?"

"Oh! Now see? That'll get you a whole lot further than that attitude shit you were giving me."

"Well, I'm sorry, daddy. It won't happen again. I promise."

"So what did she say when you talked to her?"

"She said that she promises she'll give it some thought. And she also said that she does really love you, but she's just a little hurt. She said that she needs some room to breathe for a while, and that's pretty much all she said."

"Man, all right. I'm going to hit you up later. Pick up your phone."
"What time do you plan on calling me, baby?"
"Just pick up your phone, Maria."

***

"Hey, Billy, this is Shay. I'm just calling to ask you to do something. As soon as you get up in the morning, schedule me a plane ticket—and I do mean as soon as you get up, Billy. Some crazy shit is going on down here, and I don't like it. Bye-bye." Damn, I have to get the hell out of here! I can't believe Lamont. He's crazy.

***

"Hey, Billy. Yes, I'm up. Do you have my ticket?"
"Yes, Shay I do. You have to be there in an hour."
"Thanks a lot, Billy. I'm ready to get the hell out of here."
"What's going on, Shay? Is everything OK?"
"Yeah, I'm OK, but something is going on. Lamont popped up down here."
"What? Shay, are you serious?"
"Yes, I am very serious, Billy, but let me call you when I get to the airport."
"OK, Shay. Be careful and make sure you call me when you get there."
"I will, Billy. I promise."

I have to get my shit and get out of here now! Where're my pants? I can't believe Lamont. He is absolutely crazy.
"Yes, hello! This is Shay from cabin two-oh-five. Can you send around a car to help me with my things?"

Let me make sure I have everything. Oh, I can't forget you, Mr. Vibrator.
[Someone bangs furiously on LaShay's cabin door.]
"Wait one moment. I'm coming. Please wait. Lamont, what in the

hell are you doing here? I'm leaving. Move out of my way now!"

"So you think you're just going to sneak out of here on me and go tell everything?"

"Lamont, I don't have to sneak. I'm a grown-ass woman. Move. I'm going home. Yes sir, my bags are right over there, and I'm on airport transport."

"Shay, look, baby. I love you, and I'm so sorry."

"Lamont, please just let me go. It's over."

"So it's like that, Shay? You're just going to slam the door in my face. Shay, we've been together three years, and this is how you're going to end it?"

"Bye, Lamont, and never forget you ended it like this."

***

MY JOURNAL

Dear Journal:

I'm so happy to be on the plane. This has been such a crazy trip. I thought coming to Barbados was going to make my life way more worthwhile, but it's only complicated it ten million times more. I don't know who I can tell about this whole Lamont incident. What am I to do? I know that I still love him, but I don't think I can have a relationship with him any longer.

Signed: It's Time for Me to Move On Now!

***

"Thorton, this is Lamont. Do you have my jet ready to go? I'm on my way to the airport. OK, well, just make sure they have it ready for me; I really need to get back in town. Bye."

"What's up, Tank? Is everything going good out there?"

"Everything's fucked up down here, and it really has my head messed up right now. I didn't call you because I'm all the way in Barbados."

"OK, I'll call you when I land, and man please make sure you're at the airport with my car man. Last time you kept me hanging, remember you're my driver man."

"All right. Bye."

"I have to get going; I need to get Shay back."

***

"Hey, what's up, Tank?"

Be at the airport, I will be pulling up in about ten minutes. And we need to talk. It's about LaShay. I don't know yet, but I think I want her to disappear. So just be outside the airport when I get there, we need to talk."

[Lamont hangs up the phone with Tank his driver. And dials La-Shay's phone number.]

"Shay, baby, please pick up your phone. Look, I'm on my way into town now. Let's go somewhere and talk. And, baby, don't be scared. I promise it was just an accident. I love you. Call me when you land. Bye."

***

"Hey Billy, I didn't know you we're coming to the airport. You didn't have to."

"I know Shay. You told me already, but I just wanted to make sure you were OK, that's all."

"Thanks Billy. You wouldn't believe what happened in Barbados. It was just so uncalled for."

"No Shay. What happened? All I know is that you left me that voice mail, saying you were ready to get the hell out of there."

"Yes, I was. I was so fucking scared, Billy. And I never want to talk to Lamont again."

"Shay, slow down. What happened? You're not really saying anything. What really happened out there, Shay?"

"Billy, you're like one of my best friends, but I don't know if I can tell

88

anyone about this shit."

"Shay, come on. Are you serious? You should know that I won't say anything to anyone—not even Peaches—because you're my best friend. You should know by now, Shay, that I would never betray you like that or in any other type of way. I've got your back."

"Well, you'd better not Billy—that is, if you want to keep your job."

"Shay, my lips are sealed. I promise."

"Well, when I was in Barbados, I ran into Thomas."

"Who is Thomas Shay? And please don't tell me you had a one-night stand in Barbados."

"Remember my childhood friend and my little crush I told you about—Thomas Vendell?"

"Oh, yes, I remember. How could I forget with those little bedroom stories you told me about the both of you."

"So anyways, I saw him there, and we were hanging out. You know, just reminiscing about old times. Then Lamont just pops up out of nowhere just after we kissed. He went literally insane. Next thing I know, Lamont and Thomas are arguing back and forth, and then Lamont pushes him over the ledge where we were standing."

Chapter 11

❦

Backstabber

LASHAY MARIEE: Welcome back to the show. I'm your host LaShay Mariee. And just before going to break, my best friend—well, ex-best friend—was in the middle of telling the world how she's been screwing my man, Lamont Jackson. So, Maria, is there anything else you have to confess to me about yourself? I mean, are you done telling your skank—I mean, ho—of a story?

MARIA: Bitch, I don't have to tell you shit, LaShay. The only reason I'm doing this is so that Lamont and I can finally be in public together without worrying if you or someone else is going to see us. You know what, Shay? Lamont is my man, and you just need to get over it and move on.

LASHAY MARIEE: Maria, I can't believe you. I thought we were best friends. But I guess not, huh?

MARIA: Shay, Shay. Please stop with this pity party shit. Lamont is mine and that's that. I mean, don't get me wrong, I've always thought of you as a great friend. We did everything together.
About eight months ago, Lamont and I hooked up when you went out of town; I think it was when you went on your little trip to Paris. I came over to borrow your purse like you said I could, and Lamont was there. And one thing led to another, and before I knew it, he and I were making love like rabbits.

LASHAY MARIEE: So did you at least use protection?

MARIA: I won't lie to hurt you. Yes, we did use protection in the beginning, but lately I haven't been able to find a condom anywhere.

LASHAY MARIEE: What do you mean 'in the beginning' you did, Maria? There is no ending to eight months. There is only a beginning.

MARIA: Well, if that's how you want to see it, then no, we did not use protection.

LASHAY MARIEE: Wow, Maria, you really fooled me. You both did. So is that why you've been so busy lately? Is it because you've been fucking my man? So he's been paying your tab, paying your expenses as well, correct?

MARIA: Shay, I don't think that's any of your business, but just know that I don't go untaken care of.

LASHAY MARIEE: So is that all of your confession, Maria? Or do you have more?

MARIA: No, that's all, but I am really sorry. We are really sorry that it had to end this way.

LASHAY MARIEE: Maria, let me ask you this. Who do you mean by 'we'?

MARIA: Shay, I mean Lamont and I. Who else could I be talking about? I hope you didn't think I was talking about Brent's weak ass. So is everything OK between you and I, Shay?

LASHAY MARIEE: Yes, Maria. You just stay on your side, and I'll stay on mine, and we'll be more than fine.

MARIA: OK, then, if that's how you want to do it, we will.

LASHAY MARIEE: Maria Fernandez, are you now ready to put the face with the confession so the world can see who you really are?

MARIA: No, LaShay, I think I'm going to pass on that. Anyway it was not a confession to the world. It was especially for you; you just got to hear it with your fans.

LASHAY MARIEE: So that's just supposed to be it, Maria? You're that much of a skank? You can't even come out here and face me...to face me and my fans?
[The audience applauds.]

LASHAY MARIEE: Maria, I can't believe you. You and Lamont both have been so fake.

MARIA: Bitch, I'm obviously not fake, and you obviously are. Why do you think Lamont doesn't want you anymore? It's because you're a fake-ass bitch.

LASHAY MARIEE: Thank you so very much, Maria, for that. And thank you for coming to the show.

MARIA: No, Shay, thank you. And I really mean it. Thanks so much for everything, Shay.

LASHAY MARIEE: Maria, just like everything else I gave you, Lamont is going to run out as well. Bye, Maria, and thank you for coming to the show. Wow, this has been unbearable for me.
[The audience applauds.]

LASHAY MARIEE: Thank you all for being here and understanding. You all are my real, true friends. I know none of you would sleep with my man, right? So thank you, everyone, for coming to the show. And our viewers watching at home, please stay tuned to see who will be our next week's confessor. I hope it wasn't anything like this today.

NEXT WEEK ON CONFESSIONS BEHIND CLOSED DOORS...

LASHAY MARIEE: Keith Hanson will be here to confess—and I do mean to confess—it all. Mr. Hanson, once upon a time, had it all—about to win everything he ever wanted. Mr. Hanson was the star player of his basketball team, and his grades averaged a four-point-oh. So what can go wrong in his life? Tune in next Thursday to hear Keith tell it all. I can't wait to hear this.

DIRECTOR TOM: Cut. Everyone, that was great. I loved it. The ratings are rocketing. Keep up the great work, and keep bringing the drama, LaShay.

LASHAY MARIEE: I hate that trifling bitch. I swear I hate her. She's such a home wrecker, and I'm so done with her. Billy, in my dressing room now!

BILLY: I'm right behind you, Shay. I'm right behind you.

***

"Maria, what the hell is going on?"

"What do you mean, Lamont? Everything is fine. What are you talking about?"

"You know what I mean, Maria; I can hear it in your voice. Shay called me to get my things out the storage, and before she had to go on set for the show, she told me that you were there to confess something. So what did you confess? Tell me, Maria, and tell me the truth. Because I'm really about to let your ass go, and trash your ass. Don't play with me, bitch. You're fucking up my life now. What did you say?"

"*Calm down, Lamont. You're not going to talk to me like I'm trash; I'll make you and your career trash. The ball is in my court. You want to know what I really said on the show? I mean, do you really want to know, Lamont?*"

"*Yeah, bitch, I want to know, and I want to know everything.*"

"*Well, asshole, I told her—but not just her, baby, I told the whole world—that we're in a committed relationship and we are deeply in love. I told that bitch Shay that we've been sexually involved. I told her it all.*" "*Maria, what did you tell her? Please don't tell me you said that... anything but that.*"

"*Baby, what's wrong? I thought that's what we both wanted.*"

"*Maria, what the fuck else did you say?*"

"*Well, Lamont, baby, that's really it, but then her nasty ass asked me if we have sex without rubbers. She's such a freak.*"

"*So what did you say when she asked you that, Maria?*"

"*Lamont, I told the fucking truth. The show is called* **Confessions***, so that's what the hell I did—confessed. I just told her that we've been messing around for the last eight to nine months and that we are going to be together. Which is true, right?*"

"*Maria, no, no. Why would you go on national TV and say that? I did not tell you to go on that damn show and say any of that shit, now did I?*"

"*No, Lamont baby, you didn't, but I thought that it would be necessary. Baby, I'm sorry, but please don't be mad at me.*" "*Maria, we're done. Lose my number, and I mean, it.*"

"*Lamont, Lamont, baby, don't hang up.*" Fuck. Why did I do that? Why did I go on that show? Damn, I fucked my shit up.

***

MY THOUGHTS:
PART THREE

I can't believe Lamont and Maria. I feel so betrayed by both of them. I don't know how I could not tell what was going on. I can't believe this shit. Why do things like this always happen to me? She exposed every-thing that was going on with them; I look like such a fool.

***

"Shay look, baby, it's Lamont. Please pick up the phone, baby. I want to explain everything. Shay, please call me back. I love you and only you. Bye-bye. Boo, call me."

[Lamont hangs up his IPhone hoping LaShay will call back soon.]

"Jonathan, I swear I can't believe Maria's ass. I'm so pissed off at her. She told Shay everything."

"Lamont, man, I can't believe you didn't see that shit coming. You know I'm your homeboy, and Ima keep it real. You were fucking around with her best friend, man. It was bound to happen."

"Yeah, I know, man. I just did not think Shay would leave me for it. Shay's my baby, and I love her; she really did not deserve that. That girl would have done any- and everything for me, and I fucked it up. Oh, wait a minute. This is her man. Wish me luck. I'm gonna step outside."

[Lamont jumps to his feet with excitement, and runs anxiously out-side.]

"Hey, baby. Look, before you say anything, I love you."

"Lamont, I don't want to hear that 'baby' shit. I want to hear about you fucking my best friend."

"Shay, listen baby. She didn't tell you everything. She didn't tell you the truth."

"So you guys didn't fuck each other in my house? Answer me, Lamont—now!"

"Yes baby, we did, but it wasn't like that. I swear. She just started coming on to me. Shit, Maria basically threw herself at me, and I tried to stop her, baby. I really did."

"Lamont, fuck you, and stop feeding me all your lies and bullshit. You've been fucking around with her for the past eight to nine months."

How is that a mistake? Bye, Lamont. I hope you both have a great life together."

"*Shay, baby, I love you. Please don't hang up. I'm so sorry.*"

"*I had someone that I loved, but you killed him.*"

[Lamont puts his head down, and walks back in the house with his best friend Johnathan]

"*Damn it! Jonathan, I'm about to dash off right quick. I have to take care of some business, man.*"

"*All right. Hit me up on my cell phone when you're finished. OK? And Lamont, be careful, man. Don't mess up everything you've worked so hard for.*"

"*Thanks, man, but I already know how to handle her ass. She's so predictable.*"

***

"*Mom, I can't believe her. She's such a skank.*"

"*LaShay baby, listen, it's going to be OK. You need to just erase both of them out of your memory. But honey, like I told you before, you have to make your own grown-up decisions.*"

"*Mom, I know, but I really did love Lamont. [LaShay begins to cry.]*"

"*LaShay, baby, it's going to be OK. You just need to have faith in God and pick yourself back up. You have so many people rooting for you. You don't need their negative energy around you, sweetheart.*"

"*Well, thanks, Mom, for the advice. It really helped, but I'm going to go to the park or something.*"

"*OK, honey. Are you going to be fine LaShay?*"

"*Yes, Mom. I promise I'm going to be fine. I need some fresh air, that's all.*"

"*Well, call me when you get back in, honey. Bye-bye, and I love you, LaShay.*"

"*I love you too, Mom. Bye-bye.*"

***

MY JOURNAL

Dear Journal:

I feel horrible. I don't know if I'll be able to bounce back from this one. My mom said I don't need negative energy around me. So why do I feel like I do? Like I need them both and I want to make it work for all three of us? I know I sound crazy, but I just don't know what to think anymore.

Signed: Just Because I Sound Crazy, Does That Make Me Crazy?

***

Hi, you've reached the phone of LaShay Mariee. I can't come to the phone right now, but if you leave a message, I'll get back to you. Thank you and have a great day.

"Shay, look, this is Maria. Girl, I'm sorry. No man is worth our friendship. Look, I really am sorry for everything. I want us to work this out, so please just call me when you get this message. Bye, girl. You know what, Shay? I'm on my way over there. I would rather apologize to you face-to-face. I'll be right there—in about twenty minutes. Bye, and I am really sorry."

***

Hi, you've reached the phone of LaShay Mariee. I can't come to the phone right now, but if you leave a message, I'll get back to you. Thank you and have a great day.

"Hey, baby. It's Lamont again. Look, I'm sorry about everything that happened and everything that I did. It was not supposed to happen the way it did, and I'm sorry. I really am. I want to make it up to you, so I'm on my way over to your house now. I was thinking maybe we could go take a walk in the park so that we can talk. I can't wait to see you. I'll be there in about fifteen minutes. Oh, and baby, I love you so much. See you soon. Bye."

***

MY JOURNAL

Dear Journal:

I'm sitting in the park, and I see things so much clearer out here. My mother was right. I don't need their negative energy in my life any longer. I'm so done with Maria and Lamont. They don't deserve my friendship. So here's to my new life without negative energy.

Signed: They Don't Deserve Me

***

"Hey Shay, girl. What's up?"

"Hey, Billy. I'm doing much better. What about you?"

"Nothing Shay, just sitting here with Peaches. He wants to say hi to you on speaker phone."

"Hi, Peaches. Can you hear me?"

"Yes, Shay. What's going on with you, girl?"

"Nothing much, I just went for a walk at the park trying to get a lot of this shit that I've been going through off my mind, so I won't go insane."

[There's a knock at LaShay's door.]

"Wait a moment, you guys. Someone is at my door. I wonder who that could be. I'm coming. Wait a moment, please. Lamont, what are you doing here? I told you it was over, and I meant it."

"I know Shay, but I just can't give up on us. You are the best thing that ever happened to me, and I don't want to lose you, baby. I mean, can you just let me in the house so that we could at least talk this through?"

"No, Lamont. Now leave before I call the cops. We are over! You slept with my best friend."

[Maria appears in the doorway standing beside Lamont]

"Are you serious, Maria? What the hell are you doing at my house?"

"Yeah, Maria. Why the hell are you here?"

"Shay, I came to apologize about everything. I left you a voice message; I thought you knew I was on my way."

"Maria, you know that you've already fucked things up enough between me and Shay. You really just need to leave now!"

"Lamont, shut the fuck up. I'm here to apologize to my best friend."

"Maria, you're not my friend any longer. Both of you just need to leave now."

[LaShay slams her condo door]

Chapter 12

❧

He's Not Dead!

"The Unity Foundation revolves around mistreated and abused youth. This is the kind of center we need in all of our communities around the world. There are so many young adults and youth that have been molested and have no moral support after the matter. Our nation, and our people who are in the position to help, should really lend a hand. Thank you all so much for coming out to the Unity Foundation's first fundraiser banquet. We really do appreciate all of your donations. Once again, thank you all, and good night."

"Shay, that was amazing, and I loved your speech. See, I told you that you would be wonderful."

"Thanks Billy. I was so nervous up there. I mean, I was literally shaking."

"Well, Shay, you did great—to me and everyone else. So what are you about to get into right now?"

"I guess I'm going to go home and just chill out for a moment. I'm so exhausted from work and all the fundraisers I've been participating in."

"OK, well, call me and let me know you made it home safe, OK?"

"OK. Bye, Billy, and thanks for all of your help and support."

"No problem girl. You know that I'm always going to have your back. Bye-bye."

***

MY THOUGHTS:
PART FOUR

I miss Thomas; I just can't believe he's dead. I hate Lamont for this; he's so fucking crazy, and I'm done with him. I'm so tired of using this fucking vibrator. This all could have been avoided if Lamont would have just stayed in Hawaii with Maria. I just need to move on and get over the both of them.

***

"LaShay, wait up! LaShay, stop!"
"Thomas? Thomas, is that you?"
"Yes it's me, LaShay. You look like you've seen a ghost."
"I thought...but I thought you we're dead."
"LaShay, not too loud. Someone might hear you."
"Thomas, where did you come from? How did you get here?"
"LaShay, do you know somewhere quiet we could go and talk?"
"Yeah, we can go to my place. It's just right down the road. Come on, let's go."

***

MY THOUGHTS:
PART FIVE

I can't believe Thomas is alive. Calm down, LaShay girl, regain your composure. This shit is crazy. I think I'm seeing a ghost. I don't know what to do.

***

"LaShay, snap out of it. Are you OK?"
"Yes, Thomas, I'm fine. I just kind of fell into a daze for a moment."

"Well, would you like for me to get you a glass of water, soda, wine, or maybe even some vodka?"

"Thomas, it's been four months since the last time I've seen or heard anything from you, and when I did, Lamont was pushing you of that cliff. I thought you had died, Thomas."

"Believe me, I would have, but there was an even bigger cliff right below that one. I woke up in the morning and thought I was dead already."

"Well, Thomas, why didn't you call me or come by to at least let me know you were OK?"

"LaShay, I didn't want to start or be in the middle of any more trouble than I had already encountered."

"OK, I guess that's understandable. So where have you been all this time, Thomas?"

"I told you that Barbados was like my second home. So about a year ago, I purchased some real estate out there."

"Well, I don't care, Thomas. You still should have called me; I was worried sick about you."

"I just want to ask one question. How can you worry about someone you think is dead?"

"Thomas, shut up. Just know that I was worried, OK?"

"LaShay, look, I know I should have at least called you. I'm sorry, OK? So what has been going on with you and your hubby Lamont?"

"He's not my hubby anymore, and if you keep saying stuff like that, I'm going to push you over a cliff myself. I've been going through shit here, Thomas. I found out Maria and Lamont were messing around behind my back."

"LaShay, anyone who was close to you could have seen that coming."

"Was it really that obvious, Thomas?"

"Sorry to say, but yes, it was overly obvious. All the paparazzi pictures and E! News discovery shots—I thought you would have known or at least picked up on that."

"Well, who cares now? I'm done with them both, and I want to hear nothing about them."

"So does that mean you and I can really pursue one another now without any interruptions?"

"I don't know Thomas. I mean, I totally thought you were dead. A lot of the feelings I had for you got stored away. I'm sorry."

"Well, can you let me unstore them for you? Look, LaShay, I promise not to ever leave you again. I don't want any of your friends. All I want is you. You're all I've ever wanted."

"Thomas, whatever. Please don't overdo it."

"LaShay, I'm serious. You know that. But I'm not trying to rush you into anything. I just don't want you to push me away."

"Thomas, look, I don't want to push you away, and I don't want us to move to slow."

"What do you mean by that?"

"Thomas, shut up and get over here, just kiss me already."

"LaShay, we don't have to do this. It's OK if we wait. I'll be fine with that."

"Thomas, I don't want to wait. I want you, and I want you now—right now. Just follow me, Thomas, and relax."

"OK if you're sure, LaShay."

"I'm overly sure. Lay down." [LaShay shuts her bedroom door]

***

"I love you."
"I love you too."

***

[Two hours later.]
"Please don't stop."
[Sounds of explosive meltdowns are heard.]
"Yes, yes, yes!"
"Harder!"

***

"Wow, that was amazing; I haven't felt anything like that for a long time."

"You had a man. You guys did make love, right?"

"Yes, but, believe me, it was nothing like that."

"I know. It was pretty amazing, right? So where does this take us to? Where does this leave us?"

"Well, I'm pretty sure the last position we were in was doggie."

"No, LaShay, you know what I mean. Are we together, or are we fuck buddies?

"Thomas, don't turn something so good into something so bad. I didn't know we were putting a label on it. I thought we were just having fun."

"You're right, LaShay. I don't know what I was thinking. I'm so sorry."

"Look, Thomas, I know you were expecting something more, but I'm still dealing with issues and pop-ups from my last relationship, and I don't want to bring those problems into this one. I'm sorry Thomas, I really am, but I just think it'll be better this way."

"LaShay, don't worry about it. I'll be fine. It's no big deal. Seriously, just forget I asked. Well, I guess I'm going to just get out of here."

"Thomas, no. Why are you leaving? I thought we were going to chill out for a while longer. I mean, can't we play around for a minute? Please don't leave, Thomas. I really need you right now."

"LaShay, don't you think I need you right now just the same as you need me? The difference is I need you in a different way than this. Look, LaShay, I'm sorry, but I really just need to leave. I promise I will call you tomorrow. Have you seen my shorts?"

"Yes, they're right over there. Please don't put them on, Thomas."

"I'll call you tomorrow, LaShay, so we can talk. OK?"

"OK, Thomas, if that's what you want to do. Bye then."

"I love you, and get some sleep."

***

MY JOURNAL

Dear Journal:

I can't believe Thomas is not dead. I am so relieved. We had a great time together tonight. He made me feel at peace with myself, like everything was going to be OK. The sex was amazing; he gave it to me in literally every position. So tell me, why am I here alone feeling like crap?

Signed: Sex Won't Even Help

***

"Hey, Chassidy. This is Thomas. Did you take those pictures for me walking into LaShay's condo, and store them away? OK, great. Can you please bring them to the house for me? Thanks baby. I'll be there in the next twenty minutes. All right. Bye" **Shay is going to be mine or no one's at all.**

***

"Hey, Shay, it's me, Billy. I was just calling to let you know I'm pulling up now. Are you ready to go?"
"Yes, I'm just finishing up my makeup. Come upstairs for a moment."
"All right. I'm coming up now."
*[*Billy enters LaShay's house and knocks on her bedroom door.*]*
"Shay, it's me, Billy."
"Come on in, Billy. I'm in the back restroom."
"Hey LaShay, you look all dolled up. We must still be going to the office for the model castings."
"Of course we are, silly. That's why I've been calling you like crazy. I thought you had forgotten all about it."
"So how many models are we trying to find today?"
"I'm not sure, but somewhere between forty and fifty."
"What exactly are we going to be using them for this quarter?"
"Well, remember last week I told you I wanted to host a major

campaign model spread for the Unity ModelScoop Magazine*? We really need this for the company, and this will be great publicity. OK, I'm ready, wait how do I look, Billy?"*

"You look amazing Shay, and I do mean amazing. I'm telling you, you look wonderful. Please get out of the mirror. We have to go now."

***

Lamont wakes up, sliding his feet into his four-thousand-dollar pair of Versace slippers. His cell phone rings. The only thoughts he can process are the constant worries of Shay telling the world what he did in Barbados.

"Hello, Mr. Jackson," a cold, female voice whispers with a strong sense of hate.

"Who is this?" Lamont fires back.

"Turn on your TV, Mr. Jackson. Now!"

Lamont grabs the remote and hits power. There it is. All he could do was stand there in shock.

The reporter on TV says, "Top of the news this morning: billionaire Lamont Jackson seems to be in the middle of one of Hollywood's biggest love scandals yet."

Lamont says into the phone, "Who is this? I swear, if you don't tell me, I will hunt you down and—"

"You will hunt me down and what, Mr. Jackson? What? Will you do, kill me? Is that what you were going to say? I'm just kidding around, Mr. Jackson. Calm down."

"You don't know me, lady. Stop fucking calling me Mr. Jackson."

"Lower your tone. That is, if you don't want to be on the news tomorrow, revealing your hideous cliff kill." The phone disconnects.

"Hello! Hello!" **Fuck, who was that?** *Wonders Lamont. He throws his phone against the wall. As it crashes, he sees his life, his fortune, and is fifty two-point-five-billion-dollar franchise crash into pieces with it.*

I know Shay did this, *he thinks.* I knew she was going to run her mouth sooner or later. I must kill her. She's the only witness.

Chapter 13

❧

You're Invited to The Oprah Show!

"Oh my God. I can't believe what I'm reading right now."

"What, Billy? What is it?"

"You will not believe who just e-mailed me, Peaches. This is crazy."

"Who e-mailed you, Billy? Just spit it out."

"Oprah Winfrey's booking agent just e-mailed me, baby. They asked if we can make it there this week on Thursday—well, can Shay make it there this Thursday."

"Baby, that's amazing! You should call Shay right now."

"I am. Where's my phone? She's going to be so excited. She's been waiting for something big like this for so long."

***

"Hey Shay girl. What are you doing?"

"Nothing much. I'm just sitting here at my office, reviewing some pictures and filing away some old files. Why? What's up with you, Billy? You sound so upbeat today."

"Well, do you remember about three months ago I told you that I was going to put something magnificent together for your image?"

"Yes, you did. Now tell me, Billy. You know I hate surprises."

"Well, Miss Oprah Winfrey wants you to make an appearance on her show."

"Billy, are you serious?! Billy, please don't lie to me. I can't take this right now."

"Shay, calm down. I'm not lying. This is for real right now. Oprah's

booking agent just e-mailed me, and they want you there by this Thursday. They want you to be there early Thursday morning around seven a.m. for the show's run-through."

"Wow Billy! I owe you big time. I mean, you really came through for me."

"Shay this is my job, and you are my best friend. I won't let you fall. And, plus, my name is on the line as well. So we need to leave today by five. I'm going to get the tickets and our room together, then I'll call you back to give you an update on everything."

"Why don't you just schedule the tickets for tomorrow at around four in the morning, and we could just go party and maybe celebrate the great news."

"No, Shay. We can celebrate when we come back from the show. This is too important to you and your career, and I'm not about to let you mess it all up with partying. I will be there by four p.m. to pick you up. So make sure you're ready. We don't want to miss the plane."

"OK, Billy. Oh, and thanks for keeping me on track. You're so right. I need to snap back to reality."

"No problem, girl. Well, I love you. Get up out that office, and go and get dressed. We're going to Chicago."

"I know! I can't believe it. I'm so fucking excited! OK, OK, well, bye Billy. I'm going to get dressed. Love you."

Wow, this is amazing. I can't believe it. My life is already coming together just fine without the both of them. I knew my mom was right.

"Rachael, come here please?"

"Hey, what's up? Did you call me?"

"I have to go to Chicago, and I really need you to help me get packed and decide what to wear."

"Why are you going to Chicago?"

"I have an appearance on **Oprah***! Girl, can you believe it?"*

"Are you serious? LaShay, please let me know if you're teasing me. Please, girl."

"I know. I said the same thing to Billy. I was so excited, girl. I've been waiting for this."

"So, can I go, LaShay? I've been making the most sales at the store."

"I'm sorry, Rachael, but I really need you to stay and help open and close the store with Monique. You both need to split the shifts with the new girls. I'm sorry, girl, but our business still needs to be up and running. Will you be able to handle that?"

"Of course, LaShay. We'll be fine. Go have fun. And just remember to be yourself on the show, and everything will go great."

"Thanks, Rachael. I'll see you guys when I get back. Bye, girl."

[LaShay grabs her Birkin bag and dashes out the store door. She looks down in her left hand, and sees Thomas name pop up on her caller I.D]

"Hey, Thomas, what's up? Why haven't you called?"

"Nothing's up. I just called to see how you've been doing."

"What happened to you, Thomas? You haven't called, and you haven't texted me or anything. What's going on with you?"

"Look, LaShay, I got your text messages and your calls, but I do have a career, and I am a doctor. So what's on your agenda for the day? I was thinking we could maybe go out dancing tonight or out to eat at my favorite spot, Durango's."

"No thanks, Thomas. I have a plane to catch to Chicago."

"Oh, really? I love it down there. So are you going sightseeing?"

"Well, if you must know, I've been invited to sit on the couch with Oprah and talk about my foundation and my life."

"That's amazing, LaShay! So I guess that really means you don't need me now."

"What do you mean, Thomas? I never needed you; I just always wanted you."

"Do you still want me? Is there a chance that we could make this work finally?"

"Thomas, I thought we talked about this. I'm not looking for a serious relationship. I mean, a lot has been thrown on me in the last couple of months. I don't think I could bear the load of that and a relationship."

"Well, I tried. So what time do you have to head out today?"

"I need to be on the plane by four p.m. in order to make it to Chicago on time."

"OK, when do you think you'll be making it back here? I was thinking maybe we could hook up and chill out."

"I'll be back in two days, and if I want to chill, I'll call you."

"More than likely, I'll call you to come and get some of this."

"Make sure you do that; I'll be waiting for you."

"Well, I guess I'm going to get off the phone and let you get prepared for your flight."

"OK. Bye, Thomas. I will call you when I get a chance. And you'd better pick up when I get back in town. Don't leave me worrying like that again."

"I won't. I promise I'm going to answer every call. Bye."

***

MY JOURNAL

Dear Journal:

I can't believe Oprah Winfrey wants me, LaShayMariee, to appear on her show. I'm so excited I don't know how to react. This is the kind of opportunity I've been waiting for. This is my time to shine and let the industry know I'm staying here for good. Oprah is an idol I look up to, and I can't believe she wants me on her show, I can't let my family or myself down on this.

Signed: This Is My Opportunity

***

"Hey, Billy, I'm just about done here. So when will you be here?"

"I've been waiting for you to call me, Shay. Do you want me to come and get you now?"

"Well, yes, you can come me now. I'm not done getting dressed, but I should be by time you make it here."

"OK, girl, I'm on my way right now. Just give me about thirty minutes to get there."

"OK. And, Billy? I just wanted to tell you thanks for everything—like helping me with my career and being there for me like a true friend. I don't know what I would do without you."

"Shay, that's what I'm here for. Don't forget you're like my best friend. I want nothing but the best for you, girl."

"OK, Billy, thanks. Oh! And do you know if Peaches would like to come?"

"Shay, I would love for her to come, if that's fine with you. Are you sure that's cool?"

"Yes, I'm sure. But don't get me wrong. You still are going to have to be working. Because when I'm working, you're working. But we can still chill out a little bit—my treat."

"Thanks, Shay, girl. Well, let me call her and tell her the change of plans, and then we can leave. Does that sound OK?"

"Yeah, that's fine, Billy. Just call me when you're on your way over. Oh, and tell Peaches to bring those Chanel pumps that we have alike. I want us to both wear them."

"You know that's the first thing she'll put in her bag anyway, but I'll make sure to tell her. Thanks again, Shay. Bye-bye."

***

"Hey Maria, girl, it's Sasha. I was just calling to see if you wanted to get out of the house and go out to eat with me."

"I wish, girl. That sounds amazing. But I'm trying to fix my personal life, girl. I really fucked things up."

"Why, Maria? What happened?"

"You were right, Sasha. Things went totally wrong with Lamont and Shay."

"Maria, what happened? Tell me everything. I've been so worried about you; you haven't even been calling me."

"It all came out—me and Lamont's affair. The whole world knows about it, and now Lamont and Shay want nothing to do with me. I know

that this is what you said was going to happen, but I didn't want to hear your I-told-you-so speech."

"Girl, you are my best friend, and you're always going to get the I-told-you-so speech. So once again: I told you so."

[Maria and Sasha laugh.]

"Thanks for the laugh, girl. I really needed that."

"You haven't been calling, and I was really getting worried, Maria. I went to the grocery market and picked up the **UnityModels Model-Scoop Magazine** *and saw everything that was going on. I'm sorry you got hurt."*

"What the hell? It's in the magazines and stores already? When was this, Sasha? When did you get the magazine?"

"Oh, Maria, I'm sorry. I thought you already knew about it. I mean, everything is going to be fine. Don't worry about it. I'm here for you."

"No, it's not, Sasha. It's not going to be fine. I mean I know I went on the show and told the world, but I didn't think it would get in the magazines this fast."

"Maria, just take the good with the good and the bad with the bad. Do you want to hang out with me for a while? We can go have some margaritas—my treat."

"Thanks, but no thanks, Sasha. I think I'm going to just stay at home and think things through."

"OK, girl. Well, just call me if you need anything. I'm here for you."

"OK, thanks, girl. I promise I'll call you later to let you know how I'm doing."

"OK. Bye, and make sure you call me."

"I promise I will. Bye-bye." I have to fix this. I can't let it happen like this.

***

Chapter 14

❦

I'm Ready for My Close-Up…

"You guys, doesn't it look great down here? It's beautiful."

"Yes, it is. I can't believe how amazing it looks. Thanks for inviting me and Peaches, Shay."

"No problem. I mean, who else was I going to take? You both are my real friends. Wait a minute, you guys. This is my mom calling. Hey, Mom, I just landed."

"Oh, OK, dear. How was your flight?"

"It was great, Mom. Thanks for the awesome advice. It really helped me out."

"No problem, baby. I'm your mother, and I'm supposed to give you great and knowledgeable advice. Well, I love you, LaShay. And don't get into any trouble out there."

"I won't, Mom. And, Mom, I love you too. I'll call you once we leave the set of the show, OK?"

"OK, baby. Do your best. Bye-bye."

***

"Now I'm ready, you guys. Let's get going."

"Shay, how is your mother doing?"

"Oh, she is fine, Billy. She just wanted to check on me and make sure I was doing ok.

"That's great. I'm so glad to see you and your mother getting on the right track."

"Thanks, I am too. I can't remember the last time me and my mother had a fight. Everything's great between the two of us now. So, you guys, let's have some fun. All I'm ready to do is have a drink and loosen up. This shit that has been going on with Lamont and Maria has really put me on the edge about everything."

"You're going to be fine, Shay. I promise. But I was thinking that we should go to the room first and plan everything from there."

"OK, Billy that sounds great. Let's do that, but I do want a drink after."

***

Hi. You have reached Thomas Vendell. I can't come to the phone right now, but if you leave a detailed message, I'll make sure to get back to you. Thank you and have a good day.

"Thomas, it's me, Chassidy. Call me back when you get this message. Bye-bye."

[Chassidy hangs up the phone, and walk to the photo develop counter.]

"Hello, ma'am. What can I do for you today?"

"I would like these developed in color and black and white also. How long do you think this will take? I'm kind of in a hurry."

"Not that long, ma'am—just about under an hour."

"OK. Thank you, I'll be back in a few to pick them up."

[Chassidy walks out the store, and presses the talk button on her Blackberry]

"Hey, Thomas. I just dropped off the photos. They'll be done in about an hour."

"Well, why are you just now dropping them off? I told you to do that three hours ago."

"Well, Thomas, a couple of hours ago you also told me to call Lamont and fuck with him a little bit, so that's what I've been doing. Baby, please calm down. Everything's going to be OK. I promise."

"OK, I'm sorry, baby. I'm just a little anxious to get this plan going. So what happened when you talked to Lamont?"

"He was scared shitless I could totally tell that he was going to go do everything I told him to—like we need him. So if you don't mind me asking, what's been going on with you and LaShay?"

"Nothing much, which I hate, but I'm beginning to think that we're going to need to get rid of her too."

"Why? What happened with the both of you?"

"Nothing happened. She's just been pushing me away from her and shutting me down from any contact."

"So what? I'm your girl. Fuck that hoe. You and I are supposed to be on the same team, not me you, and LaShay. Plus LaShay doesn't want you. She just broke up with Lamont Jackson, Businessman of the Year. Do you really think she wants you, Thomas? I mean, honestly?"

"Chassidy, I already had her. So honestly, yes, I think she does want me again. Look, Chassidy, I know you and I are together, but just to inform you, we're only together in the crime world—you know, like Bonnie and Clyde. I'm sorry, Chassidy, but in the real world—in the really real world—we are not together."

"What did you say, Thomas? You're a fucking jerk. I can't believe you would say something like this to me. I mean, after all we have been through together and after all I'm sacrificing for you..."

"Look, Chassidy, honey, don't turn all sensitive on me. I told you when we first started out that when we decided to get out of the game, we would just go our separate ways and live our own lives without the other one involved."

"I know, but I thought we were connecting—you know, bonding."

"Yes, Chassidy, we are, and we're still going to bond, but I want to be with LaShay now. That's always been my real true love. You know that. I'm sorry, Chassidy, I really am, but I can't lie to you. That would be wrong. I want to be with LaShay."

"I thought you had plans to kill her; you wanted the both of us to get rid of her."

"I know, I know. But I was talking nonsense. I would never do that to her, unless she made me. Look, I'm sorry, but I've known LaShay since forever. All I want to do is try to get her to sign over to our team. LaShay would be the looks and you, you Chassidy will

always be my down-ass bitch, just like Bonnie. Is that cool? Are you fine with that?"

"Yes baby, that's fine. And, daddy, you need to get her on our team fast, because if you don't, I'm going to get rid of her myself."

"Shit, you don't have to worry. I'll get rid of her if she don't get in line."

Chapter 15

❧

Welcome to The Oprah Show

OPRAH: Hello, everyone, and welcome to this segment of **The Oprah Show.** *I'm your host Oprah, and today we have a wonderful and uplifting topic. Our discussion of the day is young women who have nearly been through the pits of hell but are here to tell us how their lives are after the storm. Before we went to a commercial break, we heard an amazing story by our first guest, Tamia Heartdell. Tamia was molested by her mother and father at the age of nine and was sold in exchange for money and drugs to a Hispanic family that could not have kids. Our next guest is LaShayMariee a talk show host for one of the world's greatest TV shows out right now "Confessions Behind Closed Doors." From Miami, Florida. Please give her a round of applause.*

[The audience applauds.]

OPRAH: Hi, Miss LaShay Mariee. You look beautiful.

LASHAY MARIEE: Hi, and thank you, Oprah. You look amazing as well. I just can't believe I'm standing in front of you right now; it's been a dream of mine since I was a little girl.

OPRAH: Oh, thank you. I'm flattered. Sit down and get comfortable. We have a lot to talk about. So, LaShay, how are you? How is everything mapping out for you? I see that you have been putting in a lot of work within your community, and by that I mean, with your foundation, the Unity Foundation. Can we hear a little bit about that?

LASHAY MARIEE: *Well, I began organizing the foundation about three years ago, and I love the effect that it's having on the youth worldwide. It's so very dear to my heart. I mean, I adore the youth today and what they stand for overall. They have so much strength, and I stand to encourage them to keep going.*

OPRAH: *Well, I can say that this is something all communities around America need.*
    [The audience applauds.]

OPRAH: *So, LaShay, where did it all begin? What was your journey? What did you endure up until this chapter of your life?*

LASHAY MARIEE: *Well, Oprah, I was born in Houston Texas, but I've been residing in Miami for the last seven years. Growing up being the only girl in a nine-man family was very difficult for me. My older brother began molesting me at a very young age. I was really exposed to a lot of things like: sex, missing out on school, physical abuse, things of that nature, and forced into situations. Drugs became my downfall in life; I really became strung out on numerous types of drugs.*

OPRAH: *So, LaShay, if you don't mind me asking—because I'm pretty sure the audience wants to know—what types of drugs were you dealing with and using at that time in your life?*

LASHAY MARIEE: *When I was younger, maybe around the age of fourteen, I began doing Loracets, Ecstasy, and Vicodin—just pills. When I got a little older, around the age of sixteen, I began using marijuana and cocaine while still using all the same pills.*

OPRAH: *Wow, LaShay. I just can't believe this is true. I mean, did that not strain your mind?*

LASHAY MARIEE: *Yes, Oprah, it did. But at that time in my life, I sincerely felt that I had no one to run to for help or to ask for advice.*

Growing up, I was never home; well at least I never tried to be. I hated it there. So one day I just left and never went back. I remained in school and received my high school diploma. After graduation I went on to Texas Baptist University and received my degree from there as well. I majored in business and psychology. It's always been a real passion of mine.

OPRAH: That's amazing, LaShay. Even though you went through such agony and strain in your short lifespan, you made it through. So how has life been for you these past couple of years up until now? Have you reestablished contact with your family? Or have you done something with your degree?

LASHAY MARIEE: Yes, as a matter of fact, I have gotten in contact with my family—my mother and father. It's been a wonderful and uplifting transition to have the both of them back in my life and to have a better understanding with them of our relationship.

OPRAH: Yes, that is very wonderful. So what about your business? How's that been going for you?

LASHAY MARIEE: Oh, that's coming along wonderfully, very wonderfully. The foundation is going very well; we just raised three million dollars at our last week's banquet. My model consulting company is doing very well also. The name of the company is UnityModels Franchise, and we are in the process of promoting beautiful, passionate, and dedicated models to the modeling and beauty industry. We—and by we I mean my UnityModels staff and I—try to help them see the real picture in this industry, which is that they don't have to be a size zero or a size two. We show them that it's about real, true beauty.

OPRAH: That's amazing, LaShay. And you're so young. A lot of twenty-nine-year-old young women are not doing—or not even trying to do—such amazing things as this.

LASHAY MARIEE: Thank you so much, Oprah. I strive to work very hard every day to get to an even higher point than I already am.

OPRAH: Well, thank you very much, LaShay, for coming to the show. I loved every minute of it, and I can't wait to see more of you.

LASHAY MARIEE: No, thank you so much, Oprah, for this lovely opportunity. I really enjoyed myself and can't wait to come back.

OPRAH: We can't wait to have you back. Please give her a round of applause.
[The audience applauds.]

OPRAH: Well, we're going to go to break, and when we return, I'm going to bring out that special guest I told you all about. Stay tuned. We'll be right back with more of The Oprah Show.

***

"Hi, Thomas. I just got off the set of the show, and I saw you called. What was up?"

"Yeah, I just wanted to know how everything went with the show."

"It went great. I didn't stumble. It was just such a calm environment. I mean, I loved it."

"That's great, LaShay. I'm very excited for you. So I was calling to see if we could hang out when you get back into town. I was thinking maybe we could go somewhere for dinner, a movie, and, maybe if I'm lucky, back to my place after."

"I would definitely like that a lot Thomas—all except for the last part."

"I can't deal with that. So what time do you think you'll be back in town?"

"Tomorrow around noon. So I guess I'll just call you when I land. But I have to be on the set of my show first, so I'll call you after—at around two p.m."

Chapter 16

❧

Disappear

"How was your trip, LaShay? Did you enjoy it?"

"Yes, Mom, I did. It was amazing. I thought I would be nervous, but I wasn't at all. I was way more anxious—"

"Shay, on set, please."

"Mom, they're calling me back on set, so I have to go now, but I love you."

"Love you too, baby. Call me when you get a chance. And, LaShay?"

"Yes, Mom, what is it?"

"I'm very proud of you, and I just wanted you to know that I always have been."

"Thanks, Mom. I'm glad to finally hear that. I promise I'll call you later. Bye-bye." [Shay hangs up the phone.]

"LaShay, we need you on set now. Are you ready?"

"Yes, Tom. Just give me a minute. I'm on my way now."

***

DIRECTOR TOM: OK, everyone, take your places, please. Cameras three and four, move to the right side of LaShay, please. Cameras rolling in five, four, three, two. LaShay, you're on now.

LASHAY MARIEE: Welcome to **Confessions Behind Closed Doors.** *I'm your host LaShay Mariee, and today you don't want to miss our first confessor. David Vedoe Johnson, a mafia drug dealer from Brooklyn, confesses to us all while on his deathbed. Stay tuned to hear it all from David himself.*

DIRECTOR TOM: Cut. LaShay, that was perfect. We need you to stay on set; we'll be on in two minutes.

***

"Shay, Lamont is here to see you."

"What? Please tell me you're not serious, Billy. What in the hell does he want?"

"I don't know. Please go and calm him down. He's tripping, and we don't need that type of shit on the set."

***

"Lamont, what are you doing here? You really need to leave now—like right now. You know that this is my work, Lamont. You can't just pop up here."

"Shay, baby, look, I'm sorry about everything. Just please forgive me and take me back."

"You have to be two kinds of stupid if you can even imagine that I would take you back—especially after all the heartache and pain you've caused me."

"Look, let's just go somewhere and talk about all this, please. Please, Shay, it will only take like ten minutes of your time."

"Lamont, I have to be on set now. I'm sorry. I have to go."

"OK, that's fine, but what about after you're done? Do you think we could hook up and talk about everything after?"

"OK, look, I'm not promising anything, but call me after two, and I'll let you know if I'm up for it."

"Thank you. That's all I want—a couple of minutes of your time. But I won't hold you up any longer. I love you. Bye."

"Lamont, please don't push the point. Bye."

***

LASHAY MARIEE: Hello and welcome back to **Confessions Behind Closed Doors.** *I'm your host LaShay Mariee. Before we went to break,*

David Vedoe Johnson, our first confessor, was just about to come forth and tell the world his story and why he now is on his dying bed. David, can you hear me? Are you there?

DAVID: Yes, LaShay, I'm here. And if I might say so, you look wonderful—just gorgeous. I mean, I picked up a magazine the other day and you were in it. You looked great. You absolutely made my day.

LASHAY MARIEE: Oh, that's so sweet, David. Thanks so much. So, David, let's get down to business: the truth and where everything started and stemmed from.

DAVID: Well, LaShay, I was born to a traditional Cuban mob family. I mean through blood, not none of that fake jump-in type of shit. I was the first child and first son of the chief. I grew up with killing and selling drugs already embedded in my DNA. When I turned sixteen, my family did a traditional blessing prayer for my enrollment into the front center mob squad. And that was the first day of the end of my life. My job was to watch over six of the mod squad men. When any one of them would make a bust, I had to be there to collect all the money and merchandise they brought in. Then I would bring it all to my father. I was the youngest head honcho ever in charge. Everyone but my father had to answer to me.

My father insisted that since I was so young, he and I had to have our one-on-one meetings regularly. I was only sixteen years old when I started, so I did not fully understand the power I really had in the business. T-Bone Diesel was under me. At the time I was put on as head honcho, he was twenty-nine years old already. Just imagine how he felt taking orders from a sixteen-year-old boy, the son of the head chief in charge over everything.

By the time I was seven teen years old, there had already been fifteen killings and twenty-five busts authorized by me. I mean, it's not anything at all to brag about in this world, but in my world—the mob world—they applauded me for that. Everyone respected me, and not just for being the head chief's son anymore. I proved myself.

The first time I personally remember killing someone was on my seventeenth birthday—the highest, yet the lowest, day of my life. Everything was going great. I received everything I needed to run my half of the business.

LASHAY MARIEE: If you don't mind me asking, David, what were some of the things you needed to run the half of your business?

DAVID: Just to name a few: a TEC-Nine, a Glock, and five handguns in the truck of a brand new black-on-black Bentley. Later that day all my family and I gathered at a community park we all loved. We just had some drinks there and ate. Everyone was having a great time, and all of a sudden, KC Ellis, the nephew of one of the busts I authorized, walked up to the section where all my family was at in the park. He began to fire his gun, aiming it directly at my family. In the midst of him doing that, I raced behind him with my new, fully loaded TEC-Nine and raised it to the back of his head and pulled the trigger, two, maybe three, times. That was the first time I had really ever experienced something so brutal. His blood and bits and pieces of his brain had scattered everywhere, and I had little pieces of his brain all over my face.

After that I changed, and I couldn't hide it. Everyone knew I had changed, including the head chief, my father. I just began making all the kills and busts on my own. I felt like Superman. I fell in love with the adrenaline rush of it all. When my father found out about me making the busts and doing the killings on my own, he was furious. He told me it was not my job to get my hands dirty on a bust. So I promised him that I would stop doing the killings and making the busts on my own and I would get back to the routine of things. If he only knew I was going to start doing them even more.

It got to the point that I didn't even care anymore about the whole bust operation and taking the money and merchandise. All I cared about was killing; I had become a certified killer overnight, it seemed like. My father called me into his office one day, and I knew it was serious, because my mother was there and she was not allowed in the mob facility.

She was sitting right beside him, and I could see the anger and disappointment on the both of their faces.

My father told me to sit down and shut up. He threw an envelope in my lap. I kind of figured what was in it, but I couldn't fix my mouth to say anything. My father yelled to me very loudly, "Open the fucking envelope right now, David Vedoe Johnson," When I opened the envelope, there was all the killings and busts I had done on my own over the last couple of months.

All I could do was put my head down in shame, and all my mother could do was cry and ask my father why this was happening to her son. At the end of the conversation, I was no longer head honcho of the mob. I was just my father's son again—well, until I earned his trust back.

As soon as my rank was dropped, I lost all of the respect everyone had given me when I was head honcho. T-Bone Diesel took my place as head honcho; he thought he was the shit. It was up to me to show him that he wasn't anything more than a kiss up to my father.

LASHAY MARIEE: So, David, why did you continue killing and disobeying your father's rules?

DAVID: LaShay, my father was just an asshole who thought he had all the power; I had to get rid of him. If my father was dead or he decided to step down from his chief roll, it would automatically be passed down to me. I would become head chief of the whole operation, and I was not going to stop at anything—not anything at all. My father started to treat me like shit, making me scrub the floors, wash cars, and shine shoes— all that dumb shit. I really had to get rid of him, or I had to make him step down from his position. I knew there was no possible way my father would back down from his position as head chief, so I would have to kill him.

That week I start mapping out a great plan to get my father out of the picture. First I would tell him to look into this drug house on Eleventh Street to make a bust. I told him about it for two weeks straight. I really tried to pump him up about it, when all along it was going to be me at the house waiting for him, and at the end he would be terminated and out the plan for good.

The day had finally come, and my father was ready to make the bust. There's nothing he loves more than a house full of diamonds and gold with a few bodies and a little cash on the side. He never really understood the true meaning of the mob.

LASHAY MARIEE: What, actually, is the true meaning of the mob, David?

DAVID: I can't tell you that, but what I can tell you is that he didn't know it. So he called me and told me that he was on his way to make the bust and asked me if I could watch over everything while he was out. I reassured him that I had everything under control. While waiting for him to show up, I just waited quietly in one of the abandoned back rooms. An hour passed by, then two hours passed, then it turned into three hours. And before I realized it, five hours had passed and my father still had not made it. I was beginning to grow suspicious and doubtful about the whole situation. Then all of a sudden, I began to see white lights appear at the abandoned house's windows, and I knew it was my father.

I became very anxious and began to doubt that I could pull this of, and then it hit me. I remembered a story they told when I was just a boy. It was about my father and how he may have had something to do with my grandfather's death. This is what lead to my father's rise of power. Like father, like son, and the devils here to collect his due, so come on in, Father, come on in. "Put your hands up," was the voice I heard.

I tried to sneak out the back door, but it was already too late. My father and his accomplice had already spotted me. Without any conscience, I immediately opened fire at my father and his unknown accomplice. Before I or anyone could say a word or mutter a sound, we were all caught in this hectic crossfire. None of us had time to duck or to run for cover.

By the time the sparks had cleared, my father's masked, unknown accomplice was dead, which I later found out was T-Bone Diesel. I also was shot and wounded, and as I laid beside T-Bone on the cold, abandoned floor and drenched in both of our blood, my father stood over me with one gunshot wound to his right arm.

As he stood over me with his gun cocked straight at my heart, he muttered the words, "You were always like your grandfather. He never really knew how to aim a gun. That's why I've always told you to let people aim for you." Then he shot me and disappeared through the abandoned house.

I must have passed out, because when I woke up, I looked around and realized that I was in the hospital and I wasn't dead. It felt like my spirit was totally out of my body. The doctor quietly came into the room and stood by my bed. She told me that I was very lucky and that the bullet missed my heart by barely an inch. She began checking my blood and taking my temperature. I asked her what was going on with me and was I going to be OK. She said that I had been shot and I was paralyzed from the waist down. I couldn't believe it. My whole life went down the drain in a matter of seconds, and my father was still out there and still the chief of the mob.

My life began and ended horrible. So now I'm in a witness protection program, and my whole family wants to kill me. No one calls, and no one writes. Shit, everyone in this damn program is scared shitless of me.

LASHAY MARIEE: Wow, David. This is quite a confession. I think you might have toped our show's top ten confessions chart. If I might ask, David, do you regret any of the decisions you made back then, and do you wish you could take it all back?

DAVID: Yes. Yes, as a matter of fact, I do wish I would have done things a little differently. I wish I would have aimed a little higher rather than just shooting my father in his right arm.

LASHAY MARIEE: I don't understand that, David. I really don't get how you could want your father dead and gone, but yet you still acknowledge him as your father.

DAVID: Well, LaShay, in a Cuban Italian family, it's all about respect first. He will always be my father. Without his sack of jewels, I wouldn't be here.
[The audience laughs.]

DAVID: I know my father is still out there and he's watching this. And I just want to say to him that I do love him and it wasn't personal.

LASHAY MARIEE: Well, David, if it's fine with you, could we open the closed doors so that everyone can see who's really on that monitor?

DAVID: Yes, LaShay, I'm ready. You can open them now.

LASHAY MARIEE: Well, everyone, please give a warm welcome to David Vedoe Johnson. Open the doors, please.
[The doors open and the video monitor shows David. **Very pale yellow skin, with a long black braid resting on his right shoulder. David was hooked up to numerous machines.**]

LASHAY MARIEE: Wow, David. Are you OK in there? I see they have you pretty wired with tubes and needles.

DAVID: Yes, LaShay, I'm doing the best I can right now, just trying to survive. I'll admit I'm a little scared, but I'm fine.

LASHAY MARIEE: So, David, how do you feel now that you have opened the doors to your life and let the world know who you really are?

DAVID: I don't really have a comment on that, LaShay. I mean, there's really only one way that I could possibly feel about this. I'm in a fucking witness protection program, cut off and isolated from the rest of the world, so I pretty much feel like shit.

LASHAY MARIEE: Well, I'm very sorry to hear that, David. I really am. So now what? What do you plan to do with your life from here on out?

DAVID: Hopefully I could meet someone and settle down to have a family, but I doubt that now.

LASHAY MARIEE: Well, Mr. David Vedoe, thank you so much for confessing your story with us. That was very courageous of you.

DAVID: Thank you too, LaShay. I mean, I really do thank you for allowing me on your show to tell such a confession.

LASHAY MARIEE: Well, David, we hope you update us on your new journey through life, and we all wish you the best. Everyone, thank you for joining us tonight with another crazy episode of **Confessions Behind Closed Doors.** *We all wish David Vedoe a great journey, and we also want to thank you, our studio audience, for coming out to join the show with us all tonight. Thank you, everyone, and good night.*

DIRECTOR TOM: Cut. OK, everyone, that was great. But you all need to be here on Saturday morning at around ten thirty so we can be on the same page about next week's schedule change.

***

"Hey, Shay girl, what are you about to get into for the rest of the day?"

"Nothing much, Billy. I think I'm just going to meet up with Thomas, or just go home and rest for a while., Why do you ask?"

"Oh, no reason. I was just going to ask you if you wanted to go out for a night on the town with Peaches and me."

"Oh, Billy, that sounds great, but no thanks. I'm really tired and I need to get laid—as of yesterday."

[Shay and Billy laugh.]

"Shay, girl, you're so silly. Well, I guess go and get laid, and I'll handle the clubs tonight."

"OK. Bye, Billy. And Peaches and you both be safe tonight."

"You too, Shay. I love you, sweetie."

"I love you too. Bye-bye, Billy."

[LaShay hangs up the phone with Billy and is approached by the Director Tom.]

"Wait. Stop, LaShay. So what are you doing this weekend? Are you going out on the town to party?"

"No, I'm not, Tom. I haven't really been in the mood. I'm going home. Why do you ask?"

"Well, LaShay, we could really use some major publicity out there, so please just cheer up."

"OK, Tom, I'll try to get out for a while this week. And stop looking at me like that, Tom. I promise I'll get out for a while, OK?"

"OK, LaShay. Just for a bit. We could really use some more viewers for the show, the more the better."

"Tom, I said, OK, I will go. So I'm going to walk away now. Bye, Tom."

"LaShay, just remember what I said. The show is depending on you."

***

"Hey, Thomas. What are you getting into tonight?"

"Hey, LaShay. I'm fine. How are you?"

"Don't be sarcastic, Thomas. I'm just happy to hear your voice. So how are you doing, Thomas?"

"I'm fine, LaShay, thanks. So how have things been going with you?"

"Everything's fine. I've been thinking of you a lot lately, and I wanted to see you soon."

"Well, we could definitely arrange that. So when were you thinking of hooking up?"

"Right now—I mean, if you weren't to busy for me, Dr. Thomas."

"Don't be silly, LaShay. I would love to meet up with you now, but I have to run a quick errand to the house of one of my patients; he's very needy. So what about in an hour? Would that be fine?"

"That sounds amazing. I was actually driving on my way home from the set of the show, so it will take me about an hour to get home and get dressed."

"OK, well you do that, and I'll go take care of my patient, then I'll come straight over to get you. Make sure you put on something a little sexy."

"OK. Bye, Thomas, and don't make me wait for too long."

"I won't. I promise, boo; I'll make sure to make my way over there as soon as I'm done with this patient."

"OK. Bye and drive safe, OK?"

"OK, you too. Bye, and I can't wait to see you." Looks like I won't have to kill her after all.

Chapter 17

❧

Are You Sure LaShay Is OK?

"Well, Tamika, I had a wonderful time with you tonight. I mean, I really enjoyed myself. How about you?"

"I had am amazing time, Lamont. You really know how to treat a lady."

"I try my best. So are we going back to your place tonight or mine?"

"This is our first date, Lamont, and I really think that neither one of those ideas sounds like a good one. Well, you could just have the driver drop me off at home, and I don't know, maybe you could call me tomorrow."

"OK, that sounds great, Tamika. So I'll just give you a ring tomorrow, but call me when you make it home, so I'll know you're safe. OK?"

"OK, I can do that. You'd just better not be too busy to answer, Mr. Businessman of the Year."

"I won't. I promise to pick up for the first ring. OK, Tank, you can take her wherever she needs to go, and make sure she makes it in her place safe."

"You got it, boss; there won't be even a scratch on her."

"All right, I just talked to Tank. He's going to make sure you make it home safe, OK?"

"Thanks, Lamont. Oh, and I really had fun tonight with you."

"So did I, beautiful. Now go ahead and make it home. Bye."

***

"What's up, Chassidy? Is everything going OK?"

"Yes, Thomas, everything's going just as we planned. Lamont just left the restaurant with Tamika, so everything looks fine; I'm just waiting for her to call me with all the information."

"OK, that sounds good, but I'm on my way now. So just keep an eye on him."

"Oh, and do you still have the rope and duct tape in the back of the truck?"

"Of, course, honey. I mean, that's one of the last things I would forget. Oh, and it looks like we're not going to have to kill LaShay after all."

"Why? What happened between the two of you tonight?"

"Nothing yet, but I'm supposed to be picking her up later. I guess we'll see where it goes from there."

"Wait a minute. This is Tamika on the other line."

"OK, well just call me back, baby. And, Chassidy, please don't let me down on this one. I really need you to make this happen."

"I won't. Baby, I promise I won't. Bye-bye."

[Chassidy hangs up the phone with Thomas, and click to her other line were Tamika is breathing heavily on the phone.]

"Hey, Tamika, girl, how did everything go with you and Lamont?"

"It went OK, but I don't know why you and Thomas want to hurt him. He's a pretty cool guy."

"Look, Tamika, I didn't call you up to catch feelings for the guy or to start falling in love with him. Just remember this is a job and we don't mix business with pleasure, so just stick to the plan and fall in love on your own time, all right?"

"Damn. OK, I didn't mean to get you upset. I was just making a statement, but forget I did."

"I will forget. So anyways, besides you falling in love with the guy, what else happened?"

"Well, the whole time we were together, the only thing he talked about was LaShay mostly, and about himself of course. Oh, and at the end of *the date, he tried to take me home, but that's really all that happened, and we ate, and that's it."*

"OK, thanks, Tamika. The money will be deposited in your bank tomorrow by twelve o'clock. All right?"

"All right. Thanks. Bye-bye, girl. And just call me when you need me again."

"OK. Bye-bye, and be safe out there."

***

"He's not picking up for me, Billy. Do you think he's ignoring my calls, or what is it?"

"Well, Shay boo, I really don't know. But didn't you say that he had to take care of a patient?"

"Yes, but that was like three hours—almost four hours ago. I think I might just go over there and see what's going on with him. I'm really starting to get worried. He's never done anything like this before."

"OK, well, when you get there, Shay, just please call me and let me know if you made it safely, OK?"

"OK I will, but if he's home, don't wait up, because you know the only reason I'm chasing him is to get my brains fucked out."

[Billy laughs.] "Wow, girl, you are so crazy, but I understand where you're coming from. So just call me when you get done, OK?"

"All right, I'll try to do that, but until then, I love you. And tell Peaches I said hello."

"OK, well, drive safely Shay, and we love you too. Bye-bye."

***

"Thomas, you'd better untie me now. What the hell are you doing to me! I'm telling you, if you don't untie me, you're a dead man."

"No, Lamont, I think you're more of a dead man than I am. I mean, just look at yourself. You're all tied up in a garage, not me."

"Thomas, you're supposed to be dead. What the hell is going on? I know I killed you."

"*Well, obviously I survived the fall, and now it's your turn to try and survive my little rage of a game.*"

"*Look, Thomas, please just let me go. I mean, what do you want, money? Because if you do, I'll give you all my credit cards. Just please untie me from these fucking ropes.*"

"*No, I don't want your fucking money, and since you won't shut your mouth, I'm going to put this duct tape over it until you calm down, and shut the fuck up. Now doesn't that sound like a great plan?*"

"*No! No! Get away from me with that tape.*"

"*OK, now that you're all snug and comfy, I'm going to go do the same in your ex-girl's bed. Toddles.*"

[Lamont attempts to yell, "Leave her alone. You'd better not touch her."]

***

"*Hey LaShay, baby. I'm so sorry. This will never happen again. I just couldn't seem to get away from my patient. I saw your missed calls, and I got away as soon as I could. Look, I'm on my way now, so just hold tight, and hopefully you're not asleep by now. I really wanted to satisfy your needs. Anyway, I'm on my way. I'll be there in about thirty minutes, so wake up, sleepy head, and put on something a little sexy.*"

***

[LaShay pulls into Thomas's driveway, gets out of the car, and walks through his front door.]

"*Hello? Is anyone here? Thomas, it's me, LaShay. Are you here? Your door was wide open, so I just let myself in. Thomas, please quit playing games—well, unless we're playing a kinky one. I'm coming up the stairs now. Is this what the whole thing was about? Did you want for me just to come and chase you? Is that it?*"

[LaShay walks in Thomas's room and finds pictures of her and Lamont all over his wall.]

Chapter 17

"Oh my God. What the hell is this? What the fuck is going on right now? He can't be absolutely serious. I have to get the hell out of here—like right now."

[LaShay dashes down the stairs, but as she comes within just a few feet from her car, she hears a familiar voice screaming for help. She turns and immediately runs to the rescue.]

"Hello? Can you hear my voice? Just keep making noise; I'm trying to find you."
[LaShay opens the door to Thomas's garage and turns on the light.]
"Lamont, what the hell is going on? And what are you doing tied up in Thomas's garage?"

[LaShay walks closer to Lamont, and snatches the duct tape off of his mouth]

"Where is he? Where in the hell is he? I promise I'm going to kill him. He's insane! Wait a minute. You both planned this. I know it. You're in on it, aren't you?"
"What are you talking about, Lamont? We both planned this? Planned what?"
"Don't play dumb. You both planned to kidnap me."
"Now are you going insane? Thomas and I had a date tonight, but he stood me up. So I just came over here to see what was really going on. Have you seen his room yet?"
"No. Why in the hell would I want to see his room?"
"He has all these articles and pictures up of you and me on his wall—and posted up everywhere else. It's like he's been watching us for the last couple of years. It's creepy. What happened to you? How'd he get you here?"
"I don't remember much. But I do remember that I was coming out of a restaurant with a friend and walking back to my car. He struck me over the head with a rock, and now I'm here. All I remember after that is waking up to him tying rope and duct tape around me. Now that I'm thinking clearly, can you please untie me from all of this?"

"OK, just be still. I'm trying to untie you as fast as I can."

"Shay, stop. Turn around. He's here!"

"Thomas! What's going on? Why are you doing all of this?"

"You're not supposed to be here, LaShay. Why did you come here?"

"Because I was starting to get worried. I thought something had happened to you. So I rushed over after four hours of waiting, but I guess it wasn't you I should have been worried about. I mean, Thomas, you're a doctor. Why would you be tying people up and posting pictures of me and Lamont all over your room?"

"Shay, watch out! He's got a gun!"

"So what, Thomas? You're going to kill us? Does that really solve all of your problems?"

"It will for now. Sit down in the chair next to your man. You both can just die together for all I care. I mean, since you're so worried about him, you can die with him too."

***

"I'm starting to get really worried about her, Peaches. She's not picking up for any of my calls, and this isn't like her to just ignore all calls and text messages."

"Do you know where that guy lives so that we could go and check things out?"

"Yeah. I really do think that I should at least go and check things out, just to make sure she's OK."

"OK, well, let's go. I want to come along."

"OK, come on, and let's get dressed. First we'll go to her house and see if she's there, and if not, we'll just head over to Thomas's house."

***

"Thomas, just let us go, and please untie me."

"You came looking for something, and you found it. I'm sorry, LaShay, but now I can't let you live. You should have just stayed home and waited

for me like I told you, but now I'm going to have to kill you—well, the both of you."

"But why, Thomas? Why are you doing this to us?"

"Well, since you really want to know, I guess I could tell you both why I want you dead. Let's see, where should I begin? There's so much to go over. Well, I've been keeping an eye on you ever since you broke up with me and left town to follow your so-called dreams. I was so upset and angry that you left me...left me to rot in that sorry-ass town by myself. So that's what fueled me through all of these years. I was there when you graduated high school; I was there when you graduated from college and business trade school. Of course I've always played the background role, so that you wouldn't know it was me, but I've always been there.

"I have pictures and videos of all those moments in your life, and you have none of mine. You totally forgot that I even existed. I remember your first Miss America beauty pageant; even though you lost, I was still so proud of you. I was there when you entered the competition for the third time and you won. I remember it like it was yesterday—all the scouts just came running up to you. And before I knew it, you were hosting your own TV show.

"Now don't get me wrong, I was so happy for you. But then you shocked me when you just totally forgot what you promised me. You said when you made it, you would always come back for me and we would be together. But then I saw you on E!News *with Mr. Businessman of the Year. LaShay this is all your fault! It's always been your fault. If you would have just come back for me like you said, I would have never had to take it this far.*

"So after I saw you had a new life and a new little boyfriend, I felt like, the hell with you, fuck you, and I was done caring for you. I began making a master plan against the both of you. I mean, you can't just go around breaking peoples' hearts and leaving them to rot by themselves, so I decided that I was going to teach you a powerful lesson. When you decided to go to Barbados, I was already in the know, thanks to my accomplice.

"I got my ticket three days before you and got a hotel so I could camp out and wait for you to get there. I knew exactly what time you would be getting off your plane, so I left my room and walked around the beach, knowing that I would eventually bump into you, and I did. I did not expect—or was it ever in my plans—for your little boy toy to pop up there and push me over that ledge.

"But at least we did get to stick to one of my big plans and make passionate love. I mean it wasn't in Barbados like I'd hoped for. But when I bumped back into you again in Miami we did. I really loved that—just being inside of you and feeling all of your love just flowing on me."

"Shay, this psycho better be lying. Please, Shay, tell me he's lying."

"I'm sorry to say it for her, but we did. And to wind this conversation down, so we can get on with the evening, I think I'm going to tell a little 'confession' of my own." [Thomas bangs his head against his gun.] *"My doctor told me I would feel this fucking way; I don't want to feel anything."*

"Thomas, please calm down. I know you can get through this, but just please let us go."

"Shut the fuck up, you little slut!"

"Don't talk to her like that!"

"Lamont, I think I'm going to have to shut you up for good."

"No! Please, please don't do it! Thomas, please stop. Just think about what you're doing. No, stop!"

[Thomas raises his gun, aiming at Lamont's right leg, and pulls the trigger. Lamont screams.]

"You shot me! You really fucking shot me, you bastard!"

"Now if you don't want to be next, I advise you to shut the hell up, LaShay Mariee. I can't believe this is the guy you ditched me for. He can't even take one little bullet without crying like a little bitch."

"Thomas, you fucking shot him! What is he supposed to do? Let's see you hold it all together after being shot in your leg."

"You know, I think I might just do that." [Thomas aims the gun at his own leg and pulls the trigger.] *"Wow, that feels so amazing. And my doctor said it wouldn't. He's suck a fucking liar. I think I'm going to be paying him a little visit after this."*

"You're crazy, man. You're a fucking psycho."

"You got that right, Lamont. So that means you know not to fuck with me. Just stay in your corner and continue crying like the little bitch you are. Now let's get back to my confession. I think you both are going to love this one. Well, when I saw that you really gave up on us, I decided to make your body give up on you. Before you even say anything, shut the hell up before I shoot you in your left leg. LaShay, you better shut your little pussy boy toy up, or else you will be the only one alive to hear this confession."

"Look, Lamont, honey. It's going to be OK. Just hang in there and try not to think about the pain. I promise we're going to get out of here and get you to a hospital. Just hang on, Lamont."

"LaShay I would suggest you not make such a big promise you can't keep. For all you know, I might just leave the both of you here to rot. So now that we're done with all of that sentimental bull crap, let's move on now please. So now where was I? Oh, I know. I was telling my own little confession to the both of you. Well, about nine months ago, which was a couple of months before I bumped into you at Barbados, I met this guy—a gay guy, actually. And we discussed a proposition that I had for him, and he agreed to that proposition. I wanted him and I to engage in certain sexual pleasures in order for me to carry out my plan with you fully. So after he and I did engage in those sexual pleasures, I knew I could go for my top goal with you."

"Thomas, what are you talking about? What plan did you have for me?"

"Well, if you don't remember, we—meaning you and I—did have sex, mighty great sex that I night bumped back into in Miami a month or two ago. Before we had sex, you went into the restroom to slip on something a little sexier, and when you did, I decided to tear a little hole in the condom. So when you came out of the restroom, the lights were out and the candles were lit. You came over to the bed and laid down right beside me. I caressed your body and kissed you from head to toe. Then you told me to put on the condom, and I told you that I had already put it on. I got on top of you and felt the inside of you pulsating against me. I felt you squeezing and throbbing for me to go deeper. So I did, and when I did,

I exploded inside of you so deep and so wet that I actually had forgotten where I was for a moment."

"Thomas, why? Why would you do something like that to me? So is that why I've been feeling sick and nauseated in the mornings? Is it that I'm pregnant? Thomas, I swear, you're a sick bastard!"

"You're so right about that. I am sick, and I don't have a father, so I am a bastard. But who gives a fuck about what you think? Anyway, let's close this confession out. I really have to be somewhere. At the beginning of my little confession, I told you that this guy and I engaged in a couple of months of sexual satisfaction, and, yes, he was gay. Well, about three years ago, he was tested for HIV/AIDS, and he tested positive. And when he and I had sex, he was already taking his HIV/AIDS medicine. So now I'm HIV positive. Just to clarify for you: I did have the HIV virus when you and I had sex when I got back to Miami. Maybe that's why you've been feeling sick." [Thomas laughs.] *"Why do you look sad, baby? Aren't you happy?"*

[LaShay screams and begins to cry.] *"Thomas, what the hell did you do to me? Thomas, please let me know you're lying. Please, Thomas?"*

"Sorry, LaShay, but no, I'm not lying. You deserve to rot, just like I'm rotting. This is all your fault. Can't you see that?"

"Oh my God. Thomas, my life is over! I'm going to kill you! Untie me now!"

"Well, finally it looks like were going to do something together—die. Too bad your little boy toy is not conscious. I think he should have heard this as well since it's going to affect his life too. Wouldn't you agree, La-Shay?"

"Thomas, I hate you. I mean, it. I fucking hate you, and I promise on my life you're going to pay for what you've done to me."

"Well, you don't have much to offer now, sweetheart. And I think I have you totally beat on the whole hate ordeal."

"Thomas, just please let me go. I have to get to a hospital. Please, Thomas."

"Sorry, honey, but I can't do that. If you get cured, I'll be in this all alone. And you wouldn't want that, now would you? So I think I've done

my damage here. I'm going to leave now and get this bullet out of my leg. But you guys have fun. OK, bye."

"Thomas, don't leave us here. Untie us at least."

"Sorry, LaShay, sweetie. I can't do that. But remember once upon a time I loved you, and now it's good-bye forever."

[Thomas walks out of the garage door and is approached by a swarm of cops and FBI agents.]

"Get on the ground, now! Right now, sir! Sir, put your hands behind your back slowly and get on the ground."

"What's the problem, officers? What did I do?"

"Sir, we heard everything. Now put your hands behind your back. Yeah, there in the garage. Go in and get them now!"

"Please help us. Please untie us, officer."

"I am, ma'am. Everything is going to be OK. We have him in custody now."

"OK. Is Lamont fine? Thomas shot him in his right leg, and he went unconscious. We have to get to a hospital now! Please, just take us both to a hospital!"

"We know, ma'am. We heard everything. Please, Joey, escort them both to a hospital now. Hurry, Joey! Let's get the gentleman in the ambulance; he's like all the way unconscious."

"Shay, are you OK?"

"Billy! Oh my God, Billy. He's crazy. I should have never come here."

Chapter 18

❧

So Am I HIV Positive?

"Shay, it's OK. Peaches and I are going to come with you, OK?"

"I can't believe that bastard gave me AIDS!"

"Shay, honey, you don't know if you have it, so don't say that. I promise you everything's going to be fine. Come on, Peaches. We're going to follow Shay in the ambulance. Let's go. We have to hurry."

***

"Are you OK, Mr. Jackson? Are you OK? Can you hear me, Mr. Jackson?"

"Where am I? What's going on? Where's Shay?"

"Mr. Jackson, everything's fine. You're on the way to the hospital. You've been shot in your right leg, and you're losing a severe amount of blood."

"What about Shay? Is she OK? Where is she?"

"She is also being transported to the hospital, sir."

"Why? Did he shoot her too? Please tell me she's not shot."

"No, Mr. Jackson. She did not appear to have any visible bullet wounds. She's being admitted for a totally different medical reason."

"What exactly are those reasons? Man, she's my girl. I need to know."

"Well, Mr. Jackson, she believes that the gentlemen who has done this to the both of you has also given her HIV."

"What…What the fuck did you just say?"

"Please calm down, Mr. Jackson. Please. The more you move, the more blood you're going to lose."

"I'm sorry, sir. I'm sorry, but I can't believe this shit. Well, are she and I both going to the same hospital?"

"Yes, sir, you are. But for now, please relax. Please."

***

"Shay, just relax, honey, and let the nurse take a sample of your blood."

"Please calm down; the sooner I take a sample, the sooner we can give you your results, OK?"

"OK, I'm sorry. I'm just so scared, ma'am. I don't know what to do."

"Everything's going to be OK. We'll make sure you're taken care of. So I took all the blood that I needed. Now you can just sit back and relax while I take this to the doctor so that he can test it for the AIDS virus. I'll be back within the next three hours, OK?"

"OK, ma'am. Thank you very much for your help."

"Just hang in there. I'm going to shut the door so you and your friends can have some privacy and talk in peace. I'll be back as soon as the results come in. In the meantime, nurse Diana will check on you periodically, OK?"

"OK. Thank you so much. We'll try to keep her mind off of that for a while."

"You guys do that; she could really use the support of her friends and family right now."

"Thanks, you guys so much for coming. I really appreciate it."

"Girl, like I told you before, we're always going to be here for you through everything."

"How did you guys know were I was? And who called the police?"

"We called the police after we went to your house and saw that someone had broken in and ripped apart everything."

"Someone broke into my place? I know it was probably Thomas."

"We thought he had broken in and kidnapped you. We were so scared, so we called the cops."

Chapter 18

"Thanks, you guys. I just can't believe he lied about everything. I don't even think he's a fucking doctor, Billy."

"It's OK, Shay. We promise everything will be fine. Just don't think about that."

"What kind of career will I have once the media finds out about all of this? My career is totally over."

"Shay, honey, your career is not over. You haven't even gotten your test results back."

"Well, you're right. So have you seen Lamont? Is he fine?"

"The last time I saw him, they were taking him away in the ambulance. I'm pretty sure he's fine, Shay. But right now you need to worry about yourself."

"I know, Thank you, guys, for supporting me. I don't know how to repay the both of you."

"Just get some rest and take some time off of work for yourself."

"The station might fire me for this, so I probably won't have a choice but to take time off."

"Shay, sweetie, you make that show what it is. Trust me, they're not going to fire you, and they're not going to find out about any of this. You have my word."

"OK. Thanks. Billy, I don't know what I'd do without you and Peaches. I mean, I have no true friends left but the both of you. Maria was fucking Lamont, Thomas tried killing me, and my life is falling apart."

"No, it's not, and stop saying that. Your life is not over, and your real true friends are here with you. Look, Shay, just take your mind off of that and try to get some rest. We'll wake you when the nurse comes back in, OK, sweetie?"

"OK. Thank you, guys. I know I need to rest for a while. I'm totally exhausted."

"Do you want us to dim the lights on our way out the room?"

"Yes, please. And thanks again, friends."

"You're welcome. But don't thank us. It is a real friend's duty to be there in times of need, no matter what. Now go to sleep. Don't worry; we'll be right outside the door if you need anything, OK?

"OK. I'm just going to try and fall asleep for a while. I'll call you guys if I need you."

"OK. Sleep tight. We'll be right by your side when you wake up."

***

"Wow, I can't believe this is happening to her, Peaches. Shay is the nicest person you or I ever met. How could God let this happen to her?"

"Baby, things happen for strange reasons, and God has a great reason. I personally feel that the test is going to come back negative and she'll be fine. Shay is a very strong person, and she would never let anything stop her, so just have a little faith."

"I know. You're right, honey. I'm just so scared for her. I can't believe that sicko did this to her. He's the biggest creep ever."

***

"Hey, Chassidy, baby. Look, I'm in the hospital right now. No, no, I'm fine, but I'm going to be going to jail for a while. I have no clue how long I will be gone, but I'm pretty sure her little homo friend Billy called the police. I told you I really don't know how long I'm going to be locked down, but I'm expecting five to ten years at the most. Chassidy, stop crying, boo. Everything's going to be fine. And remember that this doesn't stop our plan. The plan is to still to be carried out by you, baby. Right now LaShay is in the hospital with Lamont. I want you to stay on her ass. Don't let her get out of your sight. She should be getting out in a couple of days. I want you to try to find some sort of way to become friends with her.

"Just try to become the best of friends with her. And when she starts to call you and tell you everything about her and how her day has been going that means you've got her. OK, I have to go, boo. Make me proud. This is the time to use everything I have taught you. Don't let me down. Well, I love you, and I'll be giving you a call from the jail later this week, so answer all calls. OK. Bye. And, Chassidy, don't betray me, or else *you'll be the one I'm coming after when I get out. LaShay will not win; she will stay in her internal prison."*

***

"Well, is she OK in there?"

"Yes, doctor, she's fine. We tried to console her as much as we could. Well, do you have her test results?"

"Yes, I have her results in my hands. Let's go in and let her open them."

[The doctor opens the room door, and Billy and Peaches follow behind her.]

"I'm pretty sure she would want me to wake her for this. Shay, sweetie, wake up. We have your test results."

"Oh my God. What do they say?"

"We don't know. You're the only one who can actually open them. Here, just open them. Don't be afraid."

"OK, well, here it goes. [LaShay slowly opens the envelope and **indescribable look appears on her face.]"** *Oh my God, Billy! Look... Look what it says!"*

THE END

www.ingramcontent.com/pod-product-compliance
Lightning Source LLC
Chambersburg PA
CBHW021153020426
42331CB00003B/32